Dawn, Dusk and Deer

True stories from the
life of a deer hunter.

by
Emmitt J. Nelson
1999

Dawn, Dusk and Deer
First Edition – May 2000

Published by:

Nelson Consulting, Inc.
10031 Briar Drive
Houston, TX 77042

Ph 713-953-1228
Fax 713-953-1112
Email nelsonci@worldnet.att.net

Copyright © 2000 by Emmitt J. Nelson

Rights are all reserved. No copying, reproduction, recording or placement in a data file or transmitted by any means whatsoever without prior approval of
Nelson Consulting, Inc.

Printed in the United States of America

ISBN 0-9664896-1-6

Dedicated to Ginny,

The one person I love most in this life. For it was her understanding, patience and long-suffering that let this man of hers loose each fall to go to the wild to answer his call to hunt deer. A call she did not understand but one she unselfishly yielded herself to accept in a most gracious manner marking her as a lady for all times and my best friend.

Emmitt J. Nelson - 1999

In Appreciation,

Many friends over sixty years of hunting have made their own treasured contribution to this work by allowing me to share in their time in the field seeking the illusive whitetail buck. In many cases I was a guest in the hunt and for that opportunity I remain forever grateful. Some of these friends are named, and some are not. But it is with deep appreciation to them all, for their companionship in the wood, on the mountain and plain that I record these true stories of my hunting for deer.

Emmitt J. Nelson - 1999

Preface

Writing about experiences I have had and reading about the experiences others have had is something I enjoy. Over my lifetime I have enjoyed reading the works, many more than once, of exceptional authors. J. Frank Dobie, Ben K. Green and Louis L'Amour, Will Henry or Elmer Kelton, are a few whose works I have read and admire. By the names above one can see that my reading has a distinct bent to the Western part of America. Being a mechanical engineer by trade, my bent to write has found fruit in many items on the technical side of my life. On the sporting side in 1998, I completed a work three decades in process titled "Wing Shooting Lead." Short though it is, it too is somewhat technical for I apply the laws of engineering and physics to the problem of successfully taking flying birds by using the correct "lead." Within "Wing Shooting Lead" I tried in a small way to insert some entertaining reading for the shooting enthusiast.

In this work I am trying to only entertain, although for the novice hunter some small amount of hunting education might result from a reading of this book.

"Dawn, Dusk and Deer" is about memories. Fond memories. It is my belief that one of the principal things gained from deer hunting is the host of great memories that one can visit, at will, year after year. All one has to do to get into a very enjoyable conversation is find another deer hunter to share memories with. True deer hunters not only love to hunt deer but they also love to tell about and hear others tell about hunting deer.

Deer hunting is in my mind a patriotic sport. The Native Americans were here and hunting deer when Europeans arrived. The settlers then hunted deer until they were almost extinct in many parts of America. With conservation they have recovered in population. And many Americans still practice the sport of their ancestors. I do. And I like to hear the stories of other hunters and to tell the stories that came to me on my deer hunting trail.

Emmitt J. Nelson - 1999

Dawn, Dusk, and Deer

PENNSYLVANIA POCONOS

A Crowded Hunt

The Hour of Dawn

RRRIIINNNGGG!!!! The desk clerk speaks the hour has come, five am. We were soon dressed and over to the Diner for breakfast. This being opening day of the Pennsylvania whitetail deer season we found the place fairly densely populated with hunters with the same sort of ideas we had. Eggs, bacon, toast and coffee down and with lunch in hand we were soon off to the wood. What a feeling - new country, deer aplenty and good deer stands. What more could two hunters desire to achieve success.

Seven, eight, nine and ten miles slowly clicked off to our appointed road intersection and turning point. A right, then a left turn, up the steep hill, a sharp right and then more hill and we moved slowly past the first farm-house. An hour before daybreak lights were on, dogs were barking and an inquiring head peered out into the morning darkness to see two happy hunters headed for their enchanted hunting grounds.

Soon we stopped at our pre-selected spot, parked the car out of the way, gathered our gear and set out through the inky blackness of the early pre-dawn morn to our newly established deer stands. Down a dim path, we paced to our designated parting spot. With a whispered "good luck" said and a "fire three shots if in trouble" agreement made, my friend made his way to the southeast as my path pointed toward the northeast.

Across an old plowed field, I would go to the far corner and then straight out into the woods about 50 yards to my Cedar Tree with its sturdy limbs awaiting my hunting boot. Using as little light as possible from my "Eveready"™ I was soon there.

Pocono Dawn

The cedar tree was right in place and I was soon safely perched, with gun in hand, in a great vantagepoint and quite comfortable. A few minutes passed and then an ever so slight glow in the east as dawn would soon break on a bright, clear and somewhat cold fall morning in the Pocono Mountains of Eastern Pennsylvania.

Dawn, daybreak in the wild! A never to be forgotten experience! Unless one has been in the forest in the minutes before dawn you have no clue as to one of the high adventures of the hunter. And once there lingered to drink in the stillness, and to strain an ear to hear a familiar sound hoping it is the sound of a deer walking. And at dim dawn begin to see the life of the woodland rise from its night of rest and experience the silent solitude. And there longed for a return to nature and felt this soul touching thrill of the early morn in the wild that God put here on earth to be enjoyed.

As I quietly surveyed natures' awakening beauty an owl is aroused from a nocturnal vigil by a noisy, nosy squirrel. Soon several bushy tails began to play in the trees around looking for a morning morsel. The crisp air carries the call of the few winter birds that had not moved south. Down below some 25 feet in the dry leaves a flock of Pine Pheasant scurry along. All the while I was taking these mental notes, my eyes scanned the brushless and open woodland below. My ears groped through all the sound that fell upon them sorting each new one for that certain rhythmic sound that is made by deer slowly and cautiously making their way through the dry autumn leaves of the forest floor.

Wait! I did hear a faint distant walking sound; a stealthy, quiet type of sound of rustling leaves. Could it be? Was I to be so fortunate?

What would it be, buck or doe?

The Set Up

Upon arriving to live in the New York City area from Texas I immediately began to "cast" around among those I met in an effort to locate the prime hunting spots for whitetail deer.

The "casting" done might better be described as "fishing" for a place to hunt; a frequently used hunter technique. Meeting with a fair amount of success with invitations to hunt deer in Virginia, Colorado and Maine I persisted in my search. Then came one I was wishing for. An invitation to hunt in the neighboring state of Pennsylvania, which was only a three-hour drive from my New Jersey side of the Hudson River.

The Pennsylvania deer season was to open on a Monday. So my host and I decided that a get-acquainted scouting trip on the preceding Saturday would be in order. It seems that the place we were to hunt was an old family farm of about 70 acres located at the end of a little traveled farm road in the backwoods of the Pocono Mountains. The party who owned the old farm place had related stories of how the deer would come out of the woods in the summer to graze in the open fields, even when people were in full view.

Further related was that the place was not hunted at all except occasionally by one of the natives. Abandoned apple orchards and nearby cornfields offered food for the deer in the fall. It seems that many old eastern farms have apple orchards. The old apple trees continue to bear fruit year after year. It is always worm laden unless someone takes the time and trouble to spray about twice per year. Having read in outdoor publications of how the deer of the east truly love the fallen apple, the entire possibility of a heavily game populated, rarely hunted area, began to form as a vision in my mind's eye.

Now all hunters of deer have the inborn talent of forming these visions of just how a place looks after having it described by a fellow enthusiastic hunter. I had left a hunter's paradise in central Texas, where deer abounded and the call of the wild is truly heard by those who love the great outdoors of Texas. Craving to commune once again with Mother Nature as one can only do in the pursuit of the whitetail deer we anxiously waited the appointed Saturday for scouting our hunting domain. Dawn of this long awaited day found us on our way with all the food and gear we thought might, with the remotest chance, be needed in our exploration of this, now, hunter's paradise that I hoped could be compared to those of my native state. Our arrival, after stopping to buy our hunting license, was about noon. After some difficulty locating the place, we stopped at each of the neighboring farms to introduce ourselves. These local folk proved to be most cordial and friendly to us and assured us that the deer in the area were indeed a worry. A vegetable garden was impossible without high fences to keep the deer out.

Adjoining the long fields of recently harvested corn, we found very attractive woodlands with rolling hills and a magnificent view of a distant river valley. The day was cold, but we were warmly clothed, so we began our scouting. At the old farm pond, tracks revealed the deer watered there. In the nearby apple orchard, half-eaten apples lay in obvious proof that this indeed might well be a hunter's dream.

The greatest encouragement came when we jumped a rather large whitetail buck from the very edge of one of the fields. As he bounded off into the forest with tail raised high, it seemed as if an entire bail of snow white cotton had suddenly taken to hoof and was very gracefully sailing over first one obstacle then another, until he was out of sight in the brush.

Needless to say we became slightly jubilant with the prospect of getting such a trophy. On into the woods we moved and soon jumped a group of about six doe and yearling deer. We thereupon established our first deer stand atop a very sturdy and flat-topped stone fence. The area was streaked with these very large fences of stone. In dimension, I judge the average size to have been three feet wide by three to four feet tall, constructed of flat stone apparently picked out of the old, old fields that had now returned again to forest. The "rock fence" stand had a very fine vantagepoint giving an excellent open view of the wooded area all around.

From here we moved northward to spot another stand, we hoped of equal promise. In our search we attempted to climb a rather promising looking tree. My friend held my foot as I swung my other leg over a limb. As I did so, considerable weight was being carried by my rib cage on a large protruding knot. No sound came but I felt a very distinct "foomp" in my chest. Thoughts of broken ribs came to mind, but there was no pain so I, in true hunter tradition, dismissed the whole possibility from my otherwise occupied mind. But that was all for that tree. Further along we came to a large, beautiful cedar, easy to climb with substantial limbs all the way to the ground. I immediately named it the "Cedar Tree Stand" in fond memory of a tree-stand friend of mine back in Texas.

In a short time, the trimming of dead limbs was finished and, indeed, a very fine stand it was. I would be in it long before dawn Monday morning to insure a good chance for the big buck. Again thoughts of broken ribs came to mind only to be dismissed once more, since any such discovery might curtail my quest for the whitetail buck on Monday.

Stands prepared, scouting complete and a good feeling in our souls we went to the nearby town about 10 miles away, and made motel reservations for Sunday night and we were off for home. A Saturday well spent we were confident. We spent Saturday night and Sunday at home before taking to the road Sunday evening back to the land of the hunt. We arrived at the motel about mid-night and had a snack at the Diner before turning in for a quick five hours sleep. Dreams crept in and bucks were hung in all the trees in the nocturnal forest of my subconscious mind.

What would it be, buck or doe?

Well no, it wasn't either. Off to my right I spotted a hunter easing through the dry leafy woods. He came to a flat surfaced rock about 60 feet south of my tree and there he stopped. The rock was one that was flush with the surface of the ground and clear of leaves, so the noise he made was little. Even though I was in clear view if he bothered to glance upward, my decision was to stay put and perhaps he would pass on by. Pretty soon the fellow got cold so he began to pace back and forth on the rock. He had laid down his rifle over on the ground. He stopped walking long enough to blow his nose and clear his throat.

Suddenly, from down the hill in front of me and to the north, someone yelled. My neighbor picked up his gun and stood very still ready to shoot. Apparently this freshly arrived hunter-neighbor of mine had a friend who was to drive the deer up the hill in his direction. Shortly, the doe and yearling deer we had seen the Saturday before broke into the view and trotted their way up the hill to pass right under my tree. No buck was with them, so neither of us got a shot.

Not sure, but I was of the opinion that my neighbor had spotted me up in the tree. It was then that another hunter appeared off in the direction I had come and about 150 yards beyond the man next to me. It was then that I began to get upset. Counting at this point at least five hunters that were all within what was a 60-acre area. These were my hunting companion, my "flat-rock" neighbor, and the hunter 150 yards to my rear plus the fellow down the hill that did the yelling and myself. Hard to dislodge from a deer stand so soon after climbing up, I continued to quietly "stand my tree."

Apparently we were all looking for the buck that never came. The three hunters near me soon grew weary and "hollered" each other back to their car. Alone again. An hour would be required for the woodland to return to the normal peaceful state after that disruption. Patiently waiting ten minutes pass, and then twenty. A little movement around, one squirrel looked over a limb, then thirty minutes crept by. Impatience was hardest to overcome as the wildlife began to show evidence that the fright had left it and the routine of the forest returned again. Again listening for the slightest sound that would announce the presence of the long awaited buck I sat my stand. Again the sound of rustling leaves fell on my ears, and then a certain walking rhythm could be distinguished. My heart began a harder beat. Perhaps at last - - -.

No, not really. Only more disappointment came as another hunter was first heard then appeared over to my right, walking almost the exact leaf covered path of the first visitor to my area. This one made his way to the same rock, stopped and stood for a few minutes.

A magnetic rock I assumed. With the dry leaves all around it did offer a quiet place to stand. During his time on the rock in plain view if he only had glanced upward I watched him, not moving, except to blink my eyes and breath. His next move was really a surprise. Presently, he moved toward my tree and looked around, for what I wasn't sure, then he walked straight to my tree and sat down and leaned his back against the tree trunk. This was hard to believe. Of all the trees in that forest, he sought mine out and sat down under it! Some luck!

It was, I concede, a very fine looking tree.

Now - what was my next move to be? One question came to mind. Did he know I was up in the tree and if he did was he doing this for a vengeful reason? Or, my suspicions raised I thought, perhaps the first hunter went out of the wood to tell this one that a stranger was out in the old cedar tree at the end of the old field; go check him out. Discouragement was getting the best of me. More than restless by now; I was plain nervous. My decision was immediate. Get down and go hunt another spot since this one seemed so popular. Quietly unloading my rifle and slinging it over my back, as yet unnoticed by my visitor, I began to descend and as haste would have it, managed to fall the last few feet, landing on my behind just inches from my intruder. My visitor, startled as I was, expressed surprise and embarrassment and was very apologetic offering to move on to another location, so I could remain.

In talking to him I learned that he lived nearby and was out hunting with his wife and son both of whom were down the hill to the north. He further explained that he was making a circle in the area to spook the deer down the hill where they were waiting to get a shot. A very nice hunter it seemed and my earlier suspicions were groundless! Explaining that I was really quite tired and cold and I was headed back to our car to get warm.

Excusing myself with a "happy to meet'cha", the car was soon in sight. By now, adding to my count of five hunters another three for this family, bringing the total to eight was far too crowded for me.

The next two hours were spent watching the apple orchard a few yards away from inside the warmth of the car. This brought me no results except a certain comfort from being out of the cold. Having seen no more hunters, I decided to work my way up an adjoining hill to a wooded area beyond the cornfield that lay southwest from the car. In about 10 minutes the edge of the trees on the far side of the field was near. As I entered the woods I was immediately confronted with a ninth hunter right in front of me asking where the Yokum Place was and did I know in which direction the road lay? I was able to tell him the direction of the road, whereupon he turned and called a companion hunter (number 10) out of the woods. Ah ha! Looked like poachers to me. Without another word they went off toward the road as I became completely demoralized. Ten hunters in a place no larger than this farm I decided was apt to end in bloodshed other than that of the whitetail deer.

It was then I went to seek out my hunting companion at the location of his stand to tell him what had transpired and suggest that we cautiously make our way back to town before we ended up being a target rather than hunters. On my way through the woods, something moved in the underbrush directly in front of me at a distance of about 10 yards. Yes, it was another hunter, walking in a low crouch with his rifle at the ready "present arms" position, straining to see what was making the noise in the leaves ahead.

He was a friendly fellow also. Telling him I was on my way to meet a hunting pal he reported that he too, had a hunting pal down the fence a'ways to the south. My pal was off to the north, soon I was looking for him with my mental adding machine marking up two more hunters to the total making it now an even dozen!

My friend had deserted his stand. Making my way back to our parked car, I joined him in a sandwich and hot coffee. We talked of my experience and added two other hunters that he had seen early that morning that we decided were a part of the group doing the deer drive that came by my Cedar Tree Stand earlier. Fourteen!

While we were sitting in our car a white pickup truck came into view to the south of us and stopped on the old farm road we had driven in on about 100 yards from our position. A lone man got out and walked with gun in hand over the hill toward the last hunter I had seen. Soon we began to hear someone blowing a police whistle and yelling loudly. This we quickly pegged as another drive and sadly stowed our gear in the trunk of the car and headed for the paved highway.

As we went down the hill to the crossroads, we passed on the way four more hunters waiting for the fruits of a deer drive over an area already driven dry. Our estimate of the sounds we heard at the beginning of this last drive was that at least two hunters were making the noise. Counting the man in the white pickup we had seen earlier we added seven more hunters to our earlier 14 for a total of 21. Twenty-one hunters soon became 19 as we turned our car eastward toward the New Jersey border.

The weather had taken a turn for the worse and as we traveled out of the Pocono Mountains a light snow soon began to fall. As we listened to the radio, the announcer mentioned a night of heavy snow was forecast, something we did not mind leaving behind.

So a mental promise I made myself; that on getting home, I ---- uh ----- oh well, next time I'll be sure the place I hunt isn't so popular, a place where the hunters are few and far between.

Ribs? Oh yes, with increasing pain I visited the doctor the following Monday, nine days after the "foomp" occurred and the inquiring eyes of an x-ray revealed the cause of my gradually increasing chest soreness to be a separated cartilage on the right front of the rib cage. But with a rib belt that was all mended well in about a week.

I'll never forget my hunt in the Poconos. A very enjoyable outing with nature, that first hour before intruders came my way. After all, I say, they were the intruders. Though living in New Jersey, we had arrived in the wood first that opening morning of the deer season.

On reflection, seeing God's creatures awake in the early dawn in a beautiful wood was worth it all. And next time I'll try not to disturb the natives as they sit under their selected tree for a rest. And who knows but someday in the future I may read an account of the time a Pennsylvania author, yet unknown, was sitting under a nice cedar tree one beautiful fall morning in Pennsylvania's Pocono Mountains. When suddenly, without warning, he was startled out of his wits as a deer hunter with a Texas drawl fell right out of the sky nearly hitting him and giving him the fright of his life.

THE HUNTER GENE

Always a Hunter

Born a Hunter

Since I was just old enough to walk, it seems I have had an intense interest in hunting. This inclination to hunt was not passed down from father to son. For my father, never hunted. Dad was a businessman first and foremost and his entire life was spent pursuing one business venture after another. Most of the time employed by others but when he was about 40 he and Mom went into the restaurant business. My growing up years were spent in the "East Texas Piney Woods," as we called them. Our restaurant was located in the center of an active East Texas oil field, which meant we had plenty of business even though we were not the only restaurant around. For miles in any direction around our home there was wooded country all unfenced. I could roam there freely and did. Even as a pre-school youth it was common for me to roam deep into the forests around our home. Getting lost was no problem for me for I was lost but once in all those years and self recovered from that episode by noticing something very familiar in the woodland and taking bearings from it was soon home again.

My first semi-lethal weapon was a slingshot as this was the armament all boys my age had. We used them in competition and in trying to harvest game for our mothers to prepare for us. In my case it was my grandmother for my mother worked along side my father in the operation of a grocery store and boarding house before the restaurant days. Soon friends owned air rifle BB guns though I never did. We formed

19

woodland safaris to seek out small game that could be taken with such a weapon. At age 13 my parents gave me a .410 single-shot shotgun for my birthday. Birds, rabbit and squirrel were my prey. I always ate what I killed or at least tried to. Later, around age 15, a summer job gave me enough cash to purchase a clip loaded Stevens .22 rifle. It was with this rifle that my first whitetail buck was bagged. By this time in my life reading Outdoor Life was my devotion and other books on hunting. So I knew what Jack O'Conner advised about exactly where to place my shot in order to get a clean kill on a whitetail deer.

My First Whitetail Buck

Two of my pals and I were out squirrel hunting one fall Saturday morning. We were hunting the Pin Oak forests near our hometown. "Still hunting" was what we called it for we had no dog available to us to put the squirrels up trees for us. My personal hunting method, modeled off my Grandfather, was to ease along through the woods doing more stopping, looking and waiting than walking. On this occasion about mid-morning pausing in my walk off to my left I heard a noise. Glancing that direction a buck and a doe running in a slow lope came into view. They were running in a direction that would have them cross my path some 15 yards in front of my present position. All the timing in this situation was absolutely perfect though it was nothing I prepared for or knowingly did. It just happened that way. After all I was not deer hunting.

The deer must have scented me for they stopped in such a position that I could not see them not could they see me.

There was a sizable oak tree just next to me that blocked viewing by either. Easing the safety to off on my .22 and leaning forward so I could see the deer, fortune found the buck nearest to me. I remember this event in photographic detail. Aiming exactly as Jack O'Conner said; low on the right front shoulder with the line of the projectile calculated to pass through the buck's heart I fired one shot. The deer bounded straight ahead in the direction they were headed and within 30 yards were out of sight in the brush. A second or so later I heard a crashing sound. Perhaps a deer falling I thought. This gave me hope.

Progress was slow on the trail for Jack had said to wait a while before proceeding to follow the kill. Soon though I could not wait any longer so plowing through the brush just in my path lay a magnificent eight point buck. To me, it was a miracle. It could not even be a dream come true for I had not the confidence to so dream. Thrilled yet a little frightened I gutted him like the hunting books said. On examination the .22 caliber "long rifle" bullet had entered the buck just in front of his right leg, hitting no bone nor rib it passed exactly through the center of the heart. Jack O'Conner had done a good job for me. The shot was perfect. Help was going to be needed to get him out to the car.

After informing my hunting companions of my kill they were in various stages of disbelief but soon were convinced and came along to help me retrieve the buck. This was soon accomplished. We took the buck to my friend's barn where we skinned and quartered the deer. All took a share and left for our respective homes with excitement overflowing.

At this point we all became avid high school age deer hunters and we were successful in a small way. Each fall of the year one of us would kill at least one deer. Soon we graduated from high school and went our separate ways. But those memories are still vividly and fondly etched in my mind.

Time passes. College is accomplished. Little hunting was done during my college years for it took everything I could muster in the way of time and jobs for income to get through those four years for a mechanical engineering degree. But on one occasion Jack Ross and I were hunting and Jack made a fine kill of a nice buck with his Marlin 30-30. Occasional deer hunting was in large groups of hunters using deer dogs. Hunting deer with dogs may sound like it is not much fun but I do have one amazing "dog deer hunt" story I want to relate to you later on. Personally, I fancy the solitude of going it alone in the wild fending for my self in trying to outwit the wily buck.

Obtaining a place to hunt in Texas is accomplished in one of four ways. One can hunt on public land, personally owned land, the land of a friend or on land you lease specifically for deer. The latter creates substantial income for ranchers who have large acreage. My early hunting was on yet unfenced private land. But those days are long gone and all land except public land came under fence.

My first chance to be a member of a deer lease was on what we called "The Sackville Ranch" along with 29 other hunters. It cost us each $75 per year in 1956 and was a wonderful place to hunt whitetail deer.

CENTRAL TEXAS SAND

The Sackville

Deer Aplenty

The Sackville ranch lay in Franklin County, Texas, in a wooded sandy soil area replete with forage for whitetail deer. The part of the ranch we had leased was a 5000-acre segment. We had a minimum of facilities but adequate for the day. It was by no means anything other than "poor boy." Just the basics, a 12' x 40' cook shack and a 12' x 40' sleeping shack made of wood frame and corrugated sheet metal. These building sat facing each other about 70 feet apart. A fence between the two buildings on each end kept out ranch animals.

The hunting process here was each hunter searched out the terrain and found sufficient deer sign to warrant hunting there. Typically then a tree was selected and steps of wood installed to allow safe climbing. Unless of course the tree was accommodating enough to supply branches close to the ground. Up in the tree one would nail in place a combination of boards to provide a place to sit comfortably for hours at a time. Then in open season, well before dawn, each hunter would make his way to his selected tree and get into position for daylight to come.

Each of the trees I adapted for deer hunting remain etched in my memory. Personally, I considered these trees as friends who aided my hunting. Care was always taken not to damage them in such a way as to impede their health and growth. But a few, especially the cedar, did receive a substantial amount of pruning. Cedars are the best for they have limbs all the way to the ground allowing safer and easier access. They are native to the area and grew tall, so finding a nicely located cedar was a desired outcome of a stand search. To this day, 40 years later, mentioning the words "Cedar Tree Stand" to any of my hunting companions of that lease will bring nods as they recall exactly the place and tree referenced.

Dawn in a Texas Tree

Nothing is quite up to the experience of climbing a pre-selected and prepared tree deep in the forest well before daybreak and sitting there in absolute silence as the woodland awakens and dawn comes ever so slowly. First there is a faint glow on the eastern horizon, which increases in brightness minute by minute. Etched in the orange colored brightness to the east one sees all the now rather bare branches of the surrounding trees. At first one cannot even see the leafed forest floor below but as the eastern sky gradually comes alive with the beautiful colors of a fall sunrise the leaves covering the ground begin to rustle as an early rising squirrel looks for a newly fallen acorn for breakfast. The sudden swooshing sound of ducks in flight comes to my ears. Even today I still recall the steady beat of the wings of a flock of mallards passing overhead as they come whizzing by at treetop level just yards from where I am sitting. They are heading for their favorite feeding spot. With discerning ears groping through all the sound down below in the leaves I can distinguish the faint footfall of a walking animal. It sounds like a deer. Will it be a buck, or will it be an armadillo foraging for grubs. The Armadillo with long nose in the leaves slowly and noisily foraging for food can keep the suspense going. As my heart rate increases my eyes probe the open areas below for a positive identification. For a small group of deer slowly foraging in dry leaves for acorns also sounds very similar. Excited and anxious I trust I will soon know.

Yes! It is! A nice whitetail buck rapidly walking toward his destination that was likely to be the scrape I found just 20 yards to my left. There he is, beautifully made and of fine rack of eight points.

Right here some non-hunter folk will ask,

"How can you shoot such a fine and beautiful creation of God?"

My answer is, "For food."

To me there is no finer meal than one featuring properly prepared fresh whitetail venison. I like it best battered and fried. But seared in a hot skillet will be just fine. I like venison roasted with potatoes and onions but grilled on a charcoal fire is best. Seasoned with a simple salt and peppershaker will be fine for me. But whatever you do with it you have two options. Cook it briefly till just done or cook it for hours until it becomes "falling apart good." Make venison sausage and have it that way appeals to my pallet even as I write this page.

"Why harvest a whitetail?"

"To eat, to eat!"

And of course venison is a very low fat meat and thus "heart healthy."

Hunting Friends and Help

It is amazing how much help one can get from fellow hunters and most of it is on a totally unasked for voluntary basis. Friends are made of this kind of stuff. I have friends I have known and hunted with for over 40 years. Such is a rare relationship. When we get together we visit the past hunts as time once again stands still as we recall the high moments of days gone by. And laugh as we reflect on all the fond memories of the adventures shared.

The Pork Roast Meal

All who hunted on the Sackville deer lease in Franklin County, Texas, admired Mr. Erwin Frazier. We all referred to him as Mr. Frazier because somehow as friendly and unpretentious as he was you simply could not bring yourself to refer to him as Erwin; especially to his face. And if with a fellow hunter and not in his presence to refer to him as Erwin would leave your colleague in a quandary for they would likely not know of whom you were speaking.

In any case the meal story goes like this. W.B. Renfrow and I were up at the Sackville hunting at the same time that Mr. Frazier was there with Mrs. Frazier. She was not always with him but on this occasion she was. On leaving the camp this particular trip W.B. and I were going by the farm of C.C. Moore, to pick up an old jeep that I had bought from him for

$100. As we were departing the camp it was near lunchtime and we did not have time to prepare a meal nor did we have any food to eat, thinking we would stop at a restaurant.

When Mr. Frazier determined what we were about to do he and Mrs. Frazier insisted that we take the roasted pork loin with us that Mrs. Frazier had cooked at home. We finally relented after much effort resisting their favor and they insisted we take a loaf of white bread so we could have roast pork sandwiches en-route. Well for some rare and unknown reason neither of us had any kind of knife. We had left all at the camp. After getting the jeep in tow we found ourselves increasing in hunger. We finally made our sandwiches by pinching off the meat with our fingers and placing it on the bread. All I remember was this highway scenario and that I had never eaten pork roast that delicious before that day nor since. It was a grand meal prepared by a grand lady and gladly given away by she and her husband to simply feed hungry friends.

Now that you know more about my friend Mr. Frazier and his general overall personality of "you first, me second," allow me to elaborate. He was always, and I realize the full meaning of the word "always," putting the interests and needs of others at the deer camp ahead of his own. He was devoted to hunting deer and made a full year's occupation out of the sport. If you had met him in other circumstances you would not have guessed in a million years that he was even remotely interested in hunting, let alone such an enthusiastic deer hunter.

For professionally he was a highly respected banking executive with a personality that was gracious, selfless and an example of perfect humility. If one were seeking banking services they would just automatically call on Mr. Frazier for he was the epitome of one who elicited trust from others.

Hogs Aplenty

The Sackville was a prolific producer of whitetail bucks. We had 30 hunters on the Sackville Lease and year after year we would each kill our two allowed whitetail bucks. The season was not open for doe so each year we would harvest 60 whitetail bucks off our 5000-acre piece of the Sackville. I hunted there for about eight years and never failed to get my two bucks. On occasion someone would be unable to hunt enough to bag two but that was rare.

The one other animal we had plenty of but did not want was hog. While these hogs were somewhat wild, the rancher owned them and each was ear marked. Few cattle were raised on our lease. Mostly hogs. They especially liked the camp area. On one occasion on a cold winter night about 20 hogs found warmth under Calvin Powitsky's cabin. Freshly built by Calvin, a lumberman, he had not boarded up the underside of his "built-on-blocks" cabin. So the hogs found that spot as a nice warm place out of the cold rainy elements and spent the night squealing and snorting, pushing and shoving. No amount of harassment by Calvin and his boys would dislodge them from their newfound lodging so in Calvin's new cabin there was no sleep that night. They were "Sleepless in Sackville" to use a thought from a movie title.

The Moon Place

The Moon Place was the 400 plus acre farm of a Texas Pioneer. It was located in Robertson County in the Central Texas Sand country not too far from the Sackville. In the years we hunted there Mr. Moon was a retired farmer and lived on the place with his wife and her sister. Located some two miles off pavement through locked gates it was a place I would call a hunter's dream. Reached by driving down what we called "two-rut" farm roads covered overhead with the lush limbs of oaks. And lining both sides of the road was thick yaupon, a small evergreen holly bush. In the fall some of the bushes will bear a beautiful bright red berry and thus make great Christmas decoration. The leaf has no sharp points like American Holly but is thin and oval shaped. And deer forage on it when they cannot get acorns from the oaks.

Mr. Moon was an accomplished trapper and hunter. Stretched skins of coon were usually being dried on the side of his barn. He also trapped Coyotes and Bobcat to keep their population down for these were predators of his favorite game, the whitetail deer.

Old fences surrounded the place. It was all wooded except for about 150 acres in open fields that were used to raise hay for the cattle. Scattered throughout the mature forested areas were many trees where, over the decades, deer stands had been built by hunters to lie in wait for the passing of a buck. As I write of these memories I can recall five distinct trees that I made into stands for the hunt on the Moon Place. Some of these had been used in decades past by other devoted hunters but the wooded 2x4 steps nailed to the trees had to be replaced and many of the planks that had been nailed in place for a setting area. I can also remember many of the bucks I took off the Moon Place for the place was overcome with game. Equally vivid in my memories are the exciting moments experienced as I watched bucks come into view. Equally vivid are the moves I made with stealth inorder to move into shooting position. For you see when seated in a tree one cannot totally anticipate the direction from which a deer will appear. More often than not they appear walking on a path that takes them by and out of range in a brief minute. Sudden movement by the hunter seen by the deer will send them bounding off into the wood with white tail flagging. So the challenge is to move into a position to fire without alarming the buck. On occasion this re-positioning must wait until the buck is walking away when their field of vision has left you behind. Quickly then, but with certainty, one can position them selves to get off the one shot before the buck is out of view. This whole scene from start to finish will take only 60 seconds or less for the woods are dense. With adrenalin flowing and heart pounding the hunter has but the few seconds to get the game.

Mr. Moon's fees for us to hunt have been forgotten but the experiences we had there have not. It was a joy to hear Mr. Moon tell about the many times he had taken whitetail bucks. He had an exact count and I remember it as 106. Over his adult lifetime he alone had killed that many deer on his farm. Venison was one of the meats in their diet along with chicken, beef and pork.

The house was fenced and typical Texas. The REA had brought electricity in the 1930's. A front porch crossed the whole of the front. Entering the living room from the porch there were two bedrooms on the left and the kitchen and dining area was in the rear. In the early years we built a small hunting shack out by his garage which sat in front of the house about 30 yards from the front door. There were usually six of us hunting the place, plus an occasional guest.

After a few years it became plain that the aging Mr. Moon was going to have to move off his place to something closer to town. My hunting pal Bill, negotiated the purchase of the place and bought it. I can remember a great number of fun days on the Moon place. And several of my "tree friends" used for deer stands still live there though I haven't paid them a visit in 10 years or more.

Stuck

Though the Moon Place was remote it was not a place unknown to the townspeople. On one hunt I managed to get the rear wheels of my Suburban off the graveled farm road and found myself deeply embedded in Central Texas sand. The truck was stuck up to its axles. There was no way I could get the truck back on hard ground. Fortunately this happened after the Moon place had come into the modern age and had a telephone. Walking to the farmhouse I called the local wrecker service and asked for help.

The wrecker owner asked, "Where are you?"

I said, "On the Moon place."

He asked; "Are the gates locked?"

I answered, "No."

He replied, "I'll be there in 30 minutes."

And he was and with long cable and wench retrieved my Suburban from the sand and drove away $40 richer. A good deal for me I was sure.

We did take a few deer, while hunting the Moon place but mostly I liked it as a retreat with its picturesque roads and fields. You just sort of felt at home on it. Later Bill sold it but we know the owners and perhaps could hunt there again if we asked. But as all things the place has changed. But my memories of the hunts there have not changed and I sometimes hunt The Moon Place in my mind. And every year or so I fancy I can hear Mr. Moon tell the story of killing the latest of his 106 whitetail bucks.

He would say, as he acted out the event, "I was sitting there on the ground behind my brush shield when this buck came walking up. I placed the sights on his shoulder and "Tow", down he went."

THE TEXAS HILL COUNTRY

Hunting The Hills

Once an Ocean

Out west of Austin and San Antonio the landscape changes from low rolling countryside of old farms now turned cattle ranches to a more arid area known as the Texas Hill Country. The hills are of ages old limestone in an area of Texas that in another era was under water. In many places one can sit on the ground and gather from the surrounding soil tiny, perfectly preserved seashells though you are 2000 feet above sea level. Live oak, cedar and juniper make up most of the larger bushes and trees. Along picturesque rivers and streams grow centuries old cypress and cottonwood and large spreading liveoak; some with expansive limbs reaching over 100 feet in diameter. There are several varieties of oak trees, most are scrubby and short in height due to the low rainfall but they have a sort of majestic beauty and in good years will produce a prolific crop of acorns.

A Texas Hill Country Peach Orchard

This story illustrates how, on some occasions, the result of all the preparation and work leading up to the actual hunt finds some uncommonly good fortune sitting at your door. And often it is only through this "good fortune" game actually finds its way into your freezer.

The father, Gwen Ross, of a high school friend, Jack Ross, bought a small Texas Hill Country ranch when he retired.

After my wife Ginny and I were married we often visited Gwen and Mama Ross. But we seldom called him Gwen, but most always called him Papa Ross. One of the principal features of the ranch was that it had a producing orchard of Hill Country peach trees, the fruit of which are know to have a great flavor.

The 160-acre ranch had two pastures in which ran a few cows and horses. The other principal feature was that the ranch sat on the shoreline of a large Hill Country Lake good for fishing. On one fall visit to the Ross' and the ranch I managed to get a few hours in hunting for whitetail deer. The day before this hunt I searched the orchard and found a peach tree that had all the makings of a true friend. Without damage to the tree I was able to find a comfortable perch high in its hefty limbs.

Peach Orchard Dawn

The next morning well before dawn I was dressed and made the short walk of about 100 yards from the ranch house front door to the welcoming branches of my new Peach tree friend. Comfortably seated and motionless I awaited the ting of light that would soon appear in the eastern sky. The wind was calm, a cold morning blessing to be sure, if you are perched in a tree. Soon the faint light of an approaching sunrise began to light the eastern sky. As a symphony orchestra builds to a crescendo the dawn came and moved on as the sun once again began to melt the frost of a Texas Hill Country cold winter's morning. The peaches, a midsummer harvest had long since been picked but all the leaves had not yet all fallen from the branches of the surrounding trees.

Off to my left I could see very well for a great distance but to my right there was only one small area visible through sort of a peephole in the branches of the tree and its remaining leaves. The peephole allowed the clear viewing of a spot about five yards in diameter some 50 yards away. So I rotated the work of my deer hunting eyes from mostly to my left where vision was largely unencumbered to an occasional glance into the peephole through the branches to my right.

This routine went on for an hour or so. The sun was full up and I was getting hungry for a Mama Ross breakfast of ham and eggs, biscuits and gravy with good hot coffee. I also thought, occasionally of a breakfast desert of one hot biscuit, opened and covered with fresh butter and some homemade peach jam.

Getting on toward irresistible was the urge to call it a day and go to breakfast for I could smell it cooking from my tree in the orchard. And I knew, for sure it was being prepared even as I contemplated it so fondly. Even today in my mind's eye I can almost break and run to the Ross' ranch house for the memories are so fresh and pure.

Usually I say to myself in these "about to quit hunting situations" that I am going to get down if no deer is seen in five minutes. Playing this game several times over, in fact, before I lower myself from the branches of a tree or leave a stand. With such a "quit soon" notion in process I continued scanning the orchard to my left preferentially with the occasional glance to my peephole on my right.

One last time to the left then to the peephole and this time there, in plain view centered through the peephole, was a beautiful mature buck with a nice rack. My cover was great for in the limbs of the tree the buck could not see me. He stood there a long time perhaps intuitively knowing he was not alone. Of all the acres in the Peach Orchard and of all the trails the buck could have taken through the orchard and of all the spots that buck could have stopped for a few seconds, fortune had it happen to me. He stopped in my peephole exactly 50 yards from my vantagepoint. It was a beautiful coincidence of nature and I'll never forget it.

Barbecued Goat

"Papa" Gwen Ross and I arranged one fall to hunt out near Bandera in the Texas Hill Country. One thing Gwen liked was a good automobile so it was unusual if he did not own a Cadillac. His Cadillacs were of the "good used" variety and gave he and Max, his wife, many comfortable miles of transportation running the long Texas highways visiting friends and family. For in that part of Texas one can drive for long periods of time over wonderfully paved highways and not pass another vehicle. So to ride in comfort is a nice added blessing.

On this occasion we were hunting some 100 miles west of where Gwen's ranch was located. We left early in the Caddy and arrived at our lease midmorning ready to check the "lay of the land" as they say down in these parts of Texas. We were the first to arrive of some six hunters so the rancher set about preparing our supper. We assisted. The plan was to barbecue a goat.

The process went as follows. The rancher caught a fat goat with little difficulty. After it was dead he hung it by its back legs to let it bleed and he then cut a slit in its stomach near the hind legs and poured the stomach cavity full of ice cold water. After letting the goat hang a while he skinned it and cut it into pieces to fit on the barbecue pit already full of hot coals from a fire the rancher had built before we arrived. The meat was slow cooked for the next seven hours, with appropriate turning and coating with a delicious sauce. Having not had a bite to eat since a very early breakfast one need little imagination as to what happened to the goat. It was absolutely delicious.

Another memorable feature of this hunt was the shelter provided by the rancher. One very old and recently used Goat Shed. The ground was our floor and it was covered with dry goat droppings so any time we moved we stirred up all manner of dropping dust that covered everything we put in the shed in about two hours. For two nights we slept in, breathed in and consumed in our food some amount of goat dropping dust. On reflection it is not a happy memory. We were glad to get this sleeping experience behind us though the supper and the hunt went just fine.

The next two days found us after the whitetail again during which hunt I fired at and missed two very plump Tom turkeys that happened by my stand. I tried one of those "suggested by friends" neck-shots and being very excited missed cleanly. I did get a nice eight-point, five year old buck.

THE TEXAS BLUE MOUNTAINS

The Koock Ranch

The Lease

The Koock ranch is about 1700 acres in size lying across two of the semi-arid and rocky Blue Mountains about 100 miles Northwest of San Antonio. This particular range of "mountains" when compared to the Rockies would definitely be called hills. Our "Deer Lease" covers a part of two mountains and lays in the range adjacent to and South of Monument Mountain. The ranch is fenced for cattle and goats though we presently have no goats. About 30 head of whiteface cattle are the resident herd. There are three pastures that are fenced and gated so the herd can be rotated from pasture to pasture. We have an all-year lease, which means we can come and go at will throughout the year although we can only hunt deer, turkey and hogs. We do not have bird-hunting rights for quail or dove.

Deer Stands

Our hunting party has 16 hunters. Each hunter may have two locations for the placement of a deer feeder. The party manager must approve the location of all feeders with the objective being to keep them safely separated so one hunter will not be overly interfering with another. At each feeder the hunter may place a very small stand that is typically comprised of a 4'x4'x7' house equipped with appropriate windows for viewing the area around the feeder. Just large enough that one can place a comfortable chair and have room enough to stand up and handle a gun safely. The typical house sits at ground level although some are elevated to give an improved view of the immediate surroundings. So most of the hunting is from these stands. With 16 hunters and only 1700 acres we do not allow any hunter to walk the lease and hunt on foot. Nor is any hunting allowed from vehicles. Deer are best left undisturbed by miscellaneous intrusions into their habitat. Very much walking and your resident deer will become resident in a less invaded place. Feed for the feeders is corn or maize. The turkeys like maize and the deer like corn. The hogs, unfortunately like both. A hunter is free do as he chooses in operating his feeders but is expected to keep them serviced and in operation from September 1st to the following April 30th though the deer season is from the first Saturday in November to the first Sunday in January. The April 30 date is to accommodate the April Gobbler season.

Deer Feeders

A "deer feeder" on our lease is a battery operated feed dispenser on the bottom of a container. These containers can be any kind of sheet metal box or drum. The feeders on our lease are mostly standard 55 gallon drums that have been adapted with a battery operated feeding mechanism attached to the bottom of the barrel to dispense the feed using some type of timer. Timers come in ether six or 12 volt and are made by a host of different companies so it is quite common to have a number of different makes and models in service on the lease.

A feeder unit can vary widely in cost from not so costly to very expensive. All the feeders we have fit between these cost spectrums at about 20% to 40% of very expensive. There are four of us who try to assist each other in keeping the feeders filled and maintained. Both filling and maintaining feeders and timers is a more difficult task to accomplish than it may seem.

Most Feeders Have Legs

The typical feeder sits about eight feet above the ground. Just out of reach so various types of ladders are employed to get at the timers and to fill the feeders. The barrels are high enough to be just out of reach of cattle so damage cannot be inflicted. Deer Lease ladders are often accidents waiting to happen so we always have tried to be very careful. I was lucky a few times when almost falling from the ladder would have brought serious injury. Once, standing on a ladder which was leaning against a feeder with 25 pounds of corn in my hands about to be hoisted into the feeder, the ladder on which I was standing caused the feeder to start to tilt over. Only luck, agility and assistance from a fellow hunter avoided a serious fall.

Another time a short fall backwards from a ladder was a near miss when my back narrowly missed a rather sharp angle iron rod that was being used to anchor the feeder against high winds. Other less serious near misses resulted in the decision that all eight of our feeders would be the tri-pod type and have hoists for the barrel so it could be lowered for filling and cranked up when filled. Thus avoiding all use of ladders. With an outlay of not a few dollars this was accomplished over about a one-year time frame. Of course, the tripods were from two different manufacturers.

Feeder History

Andy and I started out with three feeders, all his. I bought in and acquired two others by purchase from another hunter on our lease. Andy had two different types of timers. The feeders I bought had a third type of timer. When Andy and I were later joined by Ron as a member of our mutual feeder upkeep group Ron brought a feeder with him which added a fourth type of timer. Then Bill joined our group and two more feeders were bought from a hunter leaving the lease to bring our number of feeders to eight. These last two feeders had a fifth and a sixth type of timer. At this point we had eight feeders with six types of timers. There are, it seems, always one or two of the timers that give us difficulty. Problems in setting them properly or if lightening has struck nearby two of them would simply lose their settings due to the static electricity effects.

One thing that is nice is to have all feeder timers of one type and vintage. If sought, such standardization is a process that takes time while one waits on timer attrition to take its toll. Thus using attrition avoids the large capital outlay to standardize at one time.

With all this variety it is the rule rather than the exception that once a round of filling and maintenance of the eight feeders takes place it is virtually impossible to remember just what was done to each feeder. And it seems we steadfastly refuse to keep notes. A rather long discussion can be conducted by any two hunters who have worked all morning to fill and maintain the feeders and timers in attempting to recall just what was done to each one. And usually, amusingly enough, without total agreement on what transpired. I can remember one day two of us discussed at length the functioning and maintenance which required on a certain timer. When on arriving at the feeder, the time was missing. We then recalled the timer had been removed due to malfunction seven months prior by one of the two conducting the discussion and was at home in his garage.

After about four years we still have eight feeders and with all our efforts and alterations we have reduced the number of different types of timers from six to four. Another aspect of timer operation is that the batteries lose their charge. A charge can last from 2 to 5 months. It is nice if one can have a solar cell connected to the battery to keep it charged. So we now have six solar cells in operation.

Credit in an Uncommon Way

It was the summer of 1996 when Ron and I bought our sleeping trailer up at the Koock Deer lease. It was already there thanks to the owner who moved it in the year before, slept in it two times over the season and decided he wanted to sell it. So we made the purchase. The trailer, a 22-foot Fleetwood, was in fine condition. Our next project was to move it to the location we wished it to be in and wire it for electric power. This we did during a four-day trip to the lease to set it up in its new location. We needed a lot of items from various hardware and electric supply stores to get the task done. We made at least one trip per day into either

Junction or Mason or Harper to locate what we needed. Some days we made two trips.

Now the trips are not simple affairs where you just jump into the car and drive to your destination. These trips from the lease both begin with and end with the opening and closing of seven gates.

We sometimes joke that if we were in fact living behind seven gates we doubt we would ever go to town. Seven gates all operated by the passenger getting out of the car, opening the gate; the driver drives through and waits while the passenger closes the gate and gets back into the car. Without a passenger you do it all yourself. Ron and I discussed having to live behind seven gates. In our mind's eye we see wife and self, rocking on the ranch house porch on a hot summer day when Mama says, "Papa, lets go into Mason to the DQ and get a Blizzard."

Papa replies, "Boy I sure would like a Blizzard too. But you know Ma, I sure hate to go through all those gates. Think I'll just get a cold drink of water from the well."

Back to the trailer-electrifying job: on one occasion during our four days we needed just one more breaker box. For the search it was a toss-up between Junction and Mason. With Mason a mile or two closer we chose it. On arriving in town we made inquiry about electrical supplies. We were told of two businesses that might have what we needed. The first did not have it. We drove into the parking lot of the second and parked. On entering the business we took note that the receiving room was quite large, 25 by 40 feet, say. In this room were a sofa, a rocker and some Lazy Boy type chairs all sitting facing the large plate glass window that formed part of the front wall that faced town center. A quick analysis told us that the activity of the long days involved sitting and talking and looking out that large plate glass window at what was going on in town center or at who or whom was passing by on the street. There were several people sitting in various chairs, a mixture of both women and men. One of the ladies asked what it was we needed. We answered that we needed a certain breaker box for 220-volt service. She replied that that would be Clem's (not actual name) department. As she said "Clem" she pointed out a man who rose from his chair. As he walked by us at the door he said, "Follow me."

We went into the back of the store in a sort of stock room place and we helped him look for the box. After a while we did find what we were in need of and asked about the price. He replied that the person who knew prices was not in but to talk to the lady who was the cashier. After identifying her in the group we asked what the cost might be. She looked at the box and replied that the employee who was over breaker box pricing was not in the store that day.

Bewildered a bit, thinking, "Oh no," here we go, we have found the box we need but can't buy it because it has no price and we could just see ourselves driving to Junction, a 45 mile distance, to see if one was in stock in some store over there. We asked what we could do to purchase this box today.

The answer was a complete surprise to both of us when the lady said, "Just give me your name and address and we will mail you a bill when we figure out what it costs."

We thought, what? Here we are, complete strangers obviously from the big city, in a small West Texas town and you will trust us to mail you your money? The question of course was never asked as we obliged and left with the breaker box. After a short visit to the DQ and a banana split Blizzard we made our return to the deer lease with seven gates. Sure enough about a month later the bill for the breaker box came which was paid promptly by return mail. Would not want to chance that a delayed payment might ruin our credit rating.

TRUST West Texas style! Not found in big cities! These people are a part of the Texas that once was, and to some measure still is, in many West Texas communities. They deserve our admiration and respect! I can tell you that they sure have mine.

Hard on Tires

"Two day trips" are our norm for a visit to the lease. My deer lease automobile was an '89 Chevy suburban with 150,000 miles to her credit. The very first trip I made with it to the deer lease resulted in a flat tire. Likely a mesquite thorn we said. But that was not the case. When the tire was repaired the mechanic found of all things, a dog's toenail. Yes, I am serious, a dog's toenail. Somehow this toenail came off someone's dog and embedded it's rugged self into my tire and on awakening the next morning I had my first flat on the suburban. Went home and bought some of those more rugged six ply tires. The truth is, six ply tires are no longer made. For a heavier tire you must buy a four-ply tire that is six ply rated. How do they do that? I don't know, but they charge you a six-ply price for a four-ply tire and therefore you have a six-ply tire. They do appear a bit more rugged.

A deer lease can be like a hole in the ground where you throw money. But the money that goes in that hole is not new money. It is money that would otherwise go for cures for all kinds of ailments that are ignored and lived through. For you see you can't have a deer lease and be sickly. You have to be tough to do all the things that need doing at the lease. Sickness is cast aside, you have more important things to do. The deer lease takes it's toll on time. In return it gives you something to dream of and to look forward to. And I can testify that all manner of personal illnesses are ignored by each of the hunters on our lease. Because the deer lease is something that you so enjoy doing you will do it through pain and sometimes, sheer misery. And enjoy every minute of the time you spend there. It is impossible to have a deer lease and not go to it several times a year, unless you hire someone else to take care of things. And if you do that, you take away a lot of the fun and enjoyment. On our lease we all do the work ourselves.

The Trailer AC Needed Fixin'

The trailer has its permanent home at the deer lease. It itself cost $4000 and we use it to sleep in mostly. It's nice and almost like home but is small and does require maintenance from time to time. This time it was the air-conditioner that needed repairing. It does get hot in the summertime in Mason County and it was hot this April. So hot that Ron almost had a heat stroke. He was so red in the face I was worried. Quickly I applied all the medical knowledge I learned from the Readers Digest Medical School and doused him good with ice cold water. He moaned his way through the frigid downpour and took the cold washrag and put it around his neck. In about 10 minutes he was in fine shape.

Back to the air-conditioner: it had just ceased to run one day during the fall. So we waited until the spring to get it repaired. Since the deer lease is seven gates off the paved road, we did not feel we could get a house call. So off the AC unit had to come. I mean off the trailer roof. This we accomplished with "main strength and luck." After much manhandling and allowing the AC to punch two nice little holes in the trailer roof we had it safely on the ground. We then removed the control panel from the interior of the trailer and in so doing discovered it had a loose wire. We immediately decided we had been duped by the AC devil. But not to be deterred we proceeded with our plan. We loaded the A/C in the back of the Sub and dropped it off at the trailer garage. They called to say the AC was in fine running condition and the charge was to be $26. Not bad for this day and age." We left it so long that they charged a $10 storage fee so we had to pay $36. But that was OK, they had earned it. On the next trip we picked it up and reinstalled it and found that indeed it did run perfectly and has ever since. Sometimes one does work that does not really need doing. This was one of those times.

Juniper for Habitat

The Koock Deer Lease has a wonderful experience that all encounter when trying to outwit the wily whitetail buck. The evergreen known as Juniper flourishes in the Blue Mountains of Mason County, Texas. Historians tell us that the Juniper in abundance in the Texas Hill Country was not there 150 years ago. That it was transported in from further south by nature. Juniper has an aromatic odor not unlike that of cedar and has a pleasant appearance to me. I believe it also masks the odor of man in the wild and thus the whitetail deer have a more difficult time picking up strange odors like those from fresh washed clothes and shaving lotion and odors like those common to man. Juniper is also a problem to the ranchers for each bush or small tree sucks up volumes of moisture daily which would otherwise go to the grasses which cattle, goats or sheep feed on; and deer for that matter.

So it is the purpose of many ranchers to eradicate the Juniper. They do this by sawing it down, thus creating great swaths of dead Juniper across the hills. Sometimes they even burn the stumps to insure it does not rejuvenate itself for Juniper is a hardy plant. Me, I like Juniper. I like its color, it's odor and the general esthetic value I believe it adds to the beauty of the countryside. And I have to believe that the deer like it too. Deer typically like to stay out of sight and in cover of some type and the juniper in the Blue Mountain range affords the whitetail deer abundant cover.

And I know from being an eyewitness that a certain whitetail doe likes the Juniper cover for another reason. During the mating season I witnessed a doe being harassed by an overzealous buck. The doe would run; the buck would give chase. On this occasion the doe ran around a small area dense with Juniper bushes and hid herself from the buck within the thick brushy area. The buck seemed like he knew she was in there hiding but would not enter to flush her out. He circled the Juniper a few times and went on his way.

After a little wait the doe emerged and went back to feeding with the other deer. Later I saw the same event re-enacted by the same two deer.

In order to find the bucks at the most opportune time one has to be hunting as dawn comes and as dusk sets in. These are two remarkably different journeys into something very familiar but totally unique when one is out in the Blue Mountain range. Dawn in a city neighborhood, though perhaps coming quietly, all one hears is overshadowed by the slowly increasing crescendo of the distant rumble of the city traffic. Out in the Blue Mountains dawn comes on the quite feet of the falling dew. Mornings in summer are pleasingly pleasant and cool. This coolness lasts well into mid-morning and gives one the opportunity to do physical work in the summer months without heat stress.

This same dawn comes very slow in the winter. One always arrives at the deer stand well before dawn for deer are early risers. Most often there isn't even the faint hint of the dim light of day appearing on the eastern horizon. Eyes become accustomed to the darkness and shadows of moving deer can be seen but not distinctly. One thinks they are seeing some animal move; the dark spots down at the feeder seem to move though it is too dark to see the movement itself. It is one of those times you can see better an object if you do not look directly at it. If one can stay awake for the next thirty minutes the most beautiful of all things will occur right before your eyes.

The forest primeval comes alive. Animals begin to stir; the few winter birds open up with their daily overtures. The early light begins to brighten and that which looked like one thing now becomes something else entirely as the mystery of darkness is erased by the slow emergence of the light of day.

Of course in the fall you always get a blend of beautiful colors that blend into the countryside with eye pleasing abundance. As this early morning saga unfolds the wily coon feeds on the corn there for the whitetail deer families feeding and carousing around the feeder.

At dawn the deer will be feeding unless the hogs are there. Deer will not hang around a feeder when there are hogs present. As the brightness of dawn comes the nocturnal animals, the hog and the coon soon fade into the surrounding Juniper seeking their bedding place for the day. Soon it is light enough to see clearly and the sun's rays impinge on the very tips of the surrounding Live Oak trees as if saying "Wake up, Wake up. Dawn is here again." Shadows fade and the whole scene begins to brighten and soon the sun begins to sooth the leaves into the production of oxygen.

The Morning Feed

The morning feed cycle is usually set just at daylight and will disperse corn for several seconds and stop. A second cycle can be set a few minutes later if desired. The feeding deer go about their breakfast meal in a serious manner. If, per chance, a dominant buck appears it becomes apparent to all deer there that the prime eating spot belongs to him. That is usually directly under the feeder where the corn is most plentiful. If he, for some reason, strays away and another deer takes his place he only has to indicate his displeasure and the offending deer will usually retreat quickly. Otherwise he might have to make a slight movement toward the offender to make his point and the choice spot remains vacant until he decides to return. Or on occasion he may allow a favorite doe feed there for a while. And on occasion he just might go feed beside her to show his affection and acceptance.

Other deer feed around the general area with the little ones doing a bit of play. Two smallish bucks may decide to practice being BIG and square off at each other with their fledging antlers; sparring, retreating and pushing one another around head to head. One sees no violence in this practice. Its' just practice after all. Or once in a while two older doe will find fault with one another and stand erect and flail their hoofs at one another's head. This always looks very dangerous for if one of those sharp hoof hits squarely it surely will hurt.

At my feeder the morning visit by the deer to feed goes on until what seems like an appointed time when all present, in the course of three to five minutes, leave the scene. And there will not be a deer in sight when just ten minutes ago there may have been a dozen or more. Thus the morning feed is over. But I do not despair for a buck making the rounds of his scrapes will be checking on the situation soon. Part of the mating process finds each buck preparing scrapes in a soft soil near by the feeder. These the buck routinely checks.

These will usually be under an overhanging limb that is low to the ground. The buck will run his horns into the limb and actually "mouth" the foliage leaving a saliva mark. Doe in estrus will come to these scrapes and urinate on the scrapped soil. When the buck makes his rounds he is looking for such a scent. Once a buck finds this situation he becomes totally absorbed in the mating ritual with this doe, if he can find her. And if there is not a dominant buck tending her when he does find her. It is during these times that the normally wary buck will become less cautious and the hunter has the best chance of getting a trophy.

The Black Spotted Buck

At my stand on the Koock I have been observing a young buck grow into a trophy buck. I call him Spot, the spotted buck, for when he was about two years old he was wounded high on the left shoulder, I assume by another buck, likely in antlered conflict. The healing process left a tuff a black hair at the scar. This black spot remained on the buck for three years. It was there the last time when he was a mature five years old. The last time I saw the spotted buck the spot of hair was gone but on close inspection with good binoculars you can still see hair of another coloration at the same place on his shoulder. There is also another distinguishing characteristic. He has a tail that is unlike any other buck I have seen on the Koock. I would call it bronze in color, almost a dull red.

I tell you about him to give you insight into the traits of whitetail bucks. Sometimes you can spot one of his offspring just by the unique tail color. At three years he had a magnificent eight-point rack. But I declined to take him in my kill because of his "black spot" and besides I like to take deer that are from six to seven years old. This gives prime bucks a chance to breed during their most prolific years.

As far as "pecking order" at the corn feeder is concerned, when "Spot" is at the feeder, he is the boss. Every deer present gives deference to him. Interesting, though he seems to have their respect willingly for he never has to warn other deer to be respectful of his position. In a way he is like some of the better bosses I have had in my working career. Those that are of such a unique personality will cause colleagues to just naturally be respectful of them. You know the type for they often are recognized and promoted and everyone is glad for them. The good bosses are that way. When I look at Spot I think of him that way; as a good feeder boss. He now has rights at my feeder that will allow him to come and go unharmed for his lifetime. I respect Spot. Of course that is true for my feeder. I cannot speak for my hunting colleagues.

The North Wind

At dawn the cold of a winter night slowly, very slowly, begins to give way to the sun's rays and just a touch of warmth can be felt. Not enough to remove snugly warm clothing, but as the sun rises it gives assurance that its' rising will dull the chill of the night with a bit of sun. That is, if the north wind becomes no more than a soft winter's breeze. If per chance, the "Strong North Wind" is aroused by some surging cold front from Canada, then all feeling of warmth that comes with the rays of the Sun is left to the psychological realm. For to be shielded from the frigid blast that comes on the wings of the north wind sets the deer hunter's primary priority for the morning; staying warm. You see the Blue Mountains in Mason County are not considered to be in the far north. The snowflake, while it occasionally falls, seldom finds refuge with its fellow flakes long enough to become an accumulation of snow. It comes on silently, falling beautifully from the clouds overhead only to find an inhospitable warmth lingering in the soil and just as silently continues on its melted way as drops of water quickly absorbed into the rocky soil. So while the Blue Mountains can become very cold, such cold does not frequently prolong itself upon the land. A few days perhaps then moderation comes and casual comfort can be reached without the latest clothing technology. Warmth can be found through a more traditional wool garment or two appropriately arranged in layers to contain the body's warmth.

Whitetail Deer Families

In the Whitetail Deer specie the dominant mother deer or senior doe will usually have in tow as she arrives on the scene one to four family members; sometimes more. These will typically be the female offspring up to one and one-half to two years old along with any male deer of under one-year-old. In some instances one of the females will be the self-appointed security "guard-doe" for the group. These guard types are very, very skittish and are very alert to any change in the surroundings, such as noises, odors or objects. They become a bothersome distraction for the hunter for they will almost always do more scenting and looking than they do eating. I have seen some of these "guard doe" circle a deer feeder area looking for odors. If any strange ones are discovered she will give off a loud blast of air from her nose, termed a snort, raise her flag tail and bound off to a more secure place with all the deer in sight leaving with her.

Only after some time has passed and perhaps not until the following day will that deer family return to the feeder. Other families may come to the feeder but normally without any following males, for the bucks will have been alerted by the "guard doe" and remain out of sight. I feel sorry for deer families with "guard doe" because they must suffer in general tranquility as the self-appointed guard wards them off unnecessarily again and again from familiar feeding areas. But, likewise, as a hunter I dislike them for what they do to my chances of success.

Since the mother doe may in any given year have twin fawns this makes it possible that the family group may number five or more. The females will stick together while the young buck will leave his mother as soon as he is about one year old. Males typically run in groups or solo until the doe go through the estrus cycle when the typical mature buck deer will go solo all the time. These cycles occur annually in the fall of the year in the Blue Mountains depending on the weather and other factors. And as far as the total doe population is concerned, this time of fertility can last over a period of several weeks where different doe come into estrus as others are completing their cycle. During this time bucks are on the go continuously. Seldom eating but always responding to nature's call to procreate. Buck deer are not seen very often except during this period of the year when it seems they are so intent on their biological needs that they throw their normally very cautious nature to the wind literally. They may range over a large area and travel over a routine that will take them on a ten to fifteen mile circuit. As they travel if any doe in estrus are in their area the buck will detect the odor on the wind and go to work in attempting to mate with this doe. All bucks in the area will contest that the doe belongs to them and them alone, thus bucks do a lot of power positioning. Horn, body size and individual determination finally decide which buck will win the favor of the doe in question. Often the bucks will square off in a fight of their headwear. The antlers of the buck deer are used as weapons against their adversaries. Usually the bigger buck with the largest horns wins but not always. On occasion a smaller buck with seeming more combative intensity will prevail. It is during this period of vulnerability that the hunter hopes to bag that trophy-sized buck.

Dawn and Wild Hogs

One morning as normal, I was in my deer hunting position about an hour before first light. As I alternated between dozing and peering into the blackness with my eight power binoculars I noticed several faint gray forms at the feeder. One looked very much like a very large buck. The buck was considerably larger than the average buck and I could not for sake of light see his horns except vaguely. I wanted a large point count and wide spread so I watched waiting for legal shooting time to arrive with its available light to make my decision to fire. Well before shooting time the big buck left the scene. This is not abnormal, for big bucks get to be big bucks by staying out of harms way. Only the mating instinct is strong enough to impose an altered sense of alertness and at such a time is when these fellows are generally harvested. Had there been a "ready doe" at the feeder he would have stayed. And it was that time of year so I was hopeful but to no avail. He was gone to stay gone for that day.

So the next morning I was again hoping to see Mr. Large down at the feeder well before dawn. This hope was present with full knowledge that the big buck might be miles away chasing some other doe. So it was with such a presumption that sure enough with very early peering through the darkness "with glass" I could see two forms. One, quite large and the other about half that size. The small one a yearling or doe I assumed and the large buck I had seen the day before I concluded. I anxiously waited. Frequently making a check with my binoculars to insure he was still around. With enough light it came time and when I took my next look I suddenly recognized the forms as two wild hogs, one considerably larger than the other.

Our lease agreement is, in order to keep the hog population down; we are urged to kill hogs that appear while we are hunting deer. As I mentally prepared myself to take a hog and not a buck I ran through the action required after killing the hog. Like a female she was indeed LARGE. Perhaps as much as 300 pounds of pork about to be mine. I did not want pork, but thought surely someone in our hunting group would and thus take the cleaning chore over from me. Or, lacking that, I would have to load the dead animal on a vehicle and dispose of it in some nearby draw. All the time I am thinking all this is the same time I am getting my rifle in position to fire and deciding as to a lung shot or a neck shot or a head shot. I carefully placed the gun barrel in the hog's direction, carefully flipped the safety off when the two hogs decided they were tired of being in harms way and they too decided they would depart. When hogs travel they do not walk; they go in sort of a trot between a run and a walk. They began their departure to my right which being a right hand shooter caused me to have to swing away from my balance zone of fire. I placed my eye to the scope and began my search for the trotting hogs only to discover that they trotted right out of my available field of fire and behind cover before you could say "scat."

I was at once disappointed and cheered. Disappointed in that here was a grand opportunity to cut down on the hog population by killing this giant of a mother hog and I failed; and cheered because once the hogs left I knew the deer would come back to the area. As mentioned earlier hogs and deer do not feed together. Deer are afraid of hogs and will give flight even if they hear one approaching.

So it was that dawn came on the quite foggy feet of heavy dew and the deer began to come in to feed. And I enjoyed the watching and waiting as the magic of dawn once more removed all shadows by the light of day. A large fat raccoon fed amongst the deer and as the sun light gave visibility to the feeder doves and a couple quail made stops by on their foraging rounds pick up a few bits of grain. The sun rose and warmed all of us present. And as I watched drowsiness weighed heavily on my eyelids. So it was that I was soon fast asleep.

In a little while I awoke with a start and standing unalarmed just yards away was indeed a nice replica of Mr. Big. Not "THE MR. BIG," but a nice substitute. What should I do? Do I take this nice buck? With heart pumping audibly I waited. Mr. Substitute finally eased off to my right into the cover and I did not see him again.

Ron Nearly Gets Killed by a Dead Hog

On this occasion Ron was hunting the Koock Ranch alone. He was particularly interested in getting a hog so he had his cassette tape of hog calling and the cassette player and loudspeaker. After trying various locations he selected one of the stands and set up for the kill. Sure enough he attracted a large sow that had no litter with her and managed to make a killing shot. He estimated her weight at 250 to 300 pounds. She was so large Ron said it was all he could do physically to lift first one end of her then the other upon the carrying platform that mounted in his trailer hitch receiver. This platform is fairly low to the ground so the lift was something like 12 to 14 inches. Having finally managed to get her on the carrying-rack and secured, the next stop was the lease game cleaning station.

This station constructed of two-inch pipe and secured with an iron rod so it would not tip over had been at the camp for several years. Backing his Jeep up to the cleaning station he connected the hoist into the hog's two rear legs at the knee and began to pull. The scene is with his jeep sitting up very near the cleaning-station pipe-poles Ron was pulling on the hoist rope lifting the hog off the carrying platform. When the hog was about half way up, the cleaning pole "anti-tip-over" rod fractured and the entire pole structure, hoist, hog and all with Ron underneath fell to the ground.

Ron later said he thought; "If it had not been so serious in potential for injury the entire episode would have passed for a comedy act."

He relates that in his mind's eye he could see the headlines in the local newspaper; "Dead hogs are dangerous. Hunter killed when a large hog he was butchering fell on him out at the Koock Ranch."

Not to be outdone Ron planned his way out of this predicament. The next morning he loaded the hog back on his carrying-rack and hauled her over to a friend's place about 25 miles away and negotiated an agreement that if the friend would help in the butchering Ron would give him half of the hog. Also not to be outdone the friend said he would assist if Ron would keep the half that had the bullet damage in it and allow him to have the half that was intact. Agreed.

Deer have Noses

A deer's nose is one of its three highly effective defensive weapons along with its eyes and ears. Deer have finely tuned olfactory glands. Deer have extremely sensitive noses and will take alarm at any unusual odor that is not common to the habitat. There is considerable commerce in the manufacture and sale of odor suppressants for deer hunters. Allow me to illustrate the odor sensitivity of deer with the following experience. One recent fall while hunting during late morning a soft breeze was blowing from my location directly toward a feeding buck about 50 yards away. As a test in my shielded position I carefully began peeling an orange with all the attendant liquids in the peeling becoming airborne aerosols as the peeling progressed. In about 30 seconds, the amount of time I estimated it would take for the orange aerosol odor to reach the buck, the buck did an instant departure at a high speed. He did not lift his head to sniff a faint odor he might have detected but in a flash he was there and then he was gone. Zing! He was out of there at the blink of the eye. Though I have known for a lifetime that deer are very sensitive to odors this event was an educational experience for me.

Deer and their Seeing

A deer's eyes have no cones, only rods; thus they are colorblind. A deer's color world runs the white to gray to black color spectrum. This is why when wearing blasé orange a hunter will not alarm deer that will see blasé orange as gray to black. The human eye sees blasé orange as a bright glaring color during the day but as light fades blasé orange to the human eye becomes black as well. Deer have a keen eye for movement and will take alarm on the slightest inadvertent motion thus the hunter may not move the slightest if a deer is looking your way. If movement is absolutely necessary then a very slow movement will offer the least chance for the deer to pick it up. Very slowly; like turning your head from forward to one side could take up to a minute. Sudden or even normal movement of hands or arms or body will be instantly seen from a long distance by a deer. So a successful hunter learns the skill of remaining motionless for long periods of time.

I can best illustrate this with an account of a "motion experiment" I performed a few years ago. Sitting in my stand a doe kept raising her head to look my way. Though I was largely hidden from view I had the distinct impression she was seeing something of me from forty yards away and I was not sure what. To test her sensitivity I slowly moved my hand that was hidden from view and moved only my index finger into view. She immediately fled "white-flag-up" with all the other deer around going with her.

Deer Hear Too

The ears of the whitetail deer are very sharply tuned to the regular sounds of the woodland. An identified unusual sound sends them bounding away in alarm with "snow white tails" high in the air. In contrast, if a sound is not readily identified as to source and direction, then often a deer will simply stand still with ears erect until they can determine the identity and direction of the sound. If the sound cannot be accepted as normal then the deer will leave the scene immediately.

I have experimented with sounds and deer many times trying to discern just how acute their hearing is. On these occasions I simply make a particular sound very gently, increasing in loudness until it is clear the deer is in fact hearing the sound. If the sound is a reasonable replication of a naturally occurring and non-threatening one then there is little notice taken by the deer. If on the other hand one makes a sound that mimics a potential enemy of the deer then immediate alarm is taken and the deer flee.

Sounds of a mother hog or sounds of a wildcat will send them scurrying every time. They give no attention to bird calls unless it is loud such as a gobbler making a mating call. And if the sound is simply strange such as a clicking or whistling sound then again alarm is taken. But there are two sounds if made at the right time of year one can be sure it will draw deer to the sound. These are the "grunt' and the sound of two buck fighting with their antlers. Taking a shed pair of antlers and clashing them together to mimic the sounds of a fight will attract other bucks, and doe as well, to view the fight. Bucks are so tuned into the mating season that they will approach any sound that immolates the sound of clashing antlers.

Once I was setting up a hunting position under a rather large juniper. To get in under the tree I had to break off a great number of small dead branches underneath. Here I could use the term bush for juniper do not in fact grow into what one could call a legitimate tree. But in this case it was a rather large one with branches sweeping all the way to the ground providing excellent cover. So I was busy breaking the lower dead branches and clearing out a place to sit up my stand. I had finished the work and was sitting in a camouflaged chair I had brought for the purpose. In front of me was a large piece of camouflaged burlap I had erected with thumbtacks so I was invisible to my field of view but could see very clearly through the burlap myself.

Within three minutes I glanced up and standing broadside just ten yards a way was a fine nine point buck with very high antlers. I sat there a short while longer and another eight-point buck strode into view. He progressed to the point where he sensed something unusual, perhaps smelling my scent, then this buck turned and quickly retreated. But both deer had come attracted by the sharp crack of the breaking branches that sounded like two bucks in combat. A camp story has it that a truck driver stopped on a remote road and was removing brush that had lodged in the grill of the truck. This while passing through the woods only to look up and see a buck coming rapidly on the scene thinking that the sound was again of two of his brothers in a fight for the favors of a female.

And the "grunt" is used by deer to communicate using a very low frequency grunt that is a short guttural; like "Gugugugugugugu." During the mating season bucks will come to this sound as well, thinking that a mating opportunity is in the offing.

Turkey

Turkey, feral hogs and deer are the principal game harvest candidates during the fall of the year. While rabbit are abundant deer hunters seldom take them. Some hunters will take turkeys as often as they can until the annual limit of four is taken. That happens to be my preference. Although, if I find myself engaged in attempting to take a trophy-buck, then I might allow a turkey to pass by unharmed; or at least not startled. It is not a seldom occurrence that a turkey will be missed by even the most skilled marksman.

In taking a turkey it is important that the hunter attempt to preserve the breast flesh intact. Therefore many attempt to take the turkey with a smaller caliber rifle or shotgun. I try to shoot them with my deer rifle placing the shot in the neck. A turkey's neck is about one to one and one-half inches in diameter and in fairly constant movement as they stay on the alert. So missing a turkey's neck as the most productive target is not at all uncommon. And just as important a hit in the turkey's neck is nearly always fatal.

In my experience wounded turkeys that subsequently die are a rarity when attempting neck shots. It is a hit or a miss proposition. While shooting turkeys in the body with a rifle, unless it is very small bore, will normally distroy a lot of meat or wound the turkey in such a way that they simply flee only to die later.

Wild turkeys are very hardy birds and not easy to kill. Any hunter can tell you tales of turkey that were lying dead only to get see them get up and escape. I once was deer hunting out west of the Blue Mountains when a "get up and flee" turkey event came my way. On the occasion I am relating I was in a tree looking to kill a nice buck when some 150 yards away I spied about 10 large turkeys running in a large open area as if they were spooked by another hunter. I decided to try to get the lead Tom before they moved from my view at about 100 yards distance as they were running quartering in my direction. As they ran I took careful aim giving the approximate amount of lead and fired. Down went the lead turkey in a cloud of feathers. A very good shot I concluded.

As luck would have it the turkeys flew in all directions and one of them flew right to me and landed not 20 yards away off to my left. I easily put a shot right into the bird's body chancing there would be some meat left. That turkey too fell right where I shot it. Seeing both turkeys prostrate on the ground I carefully made my way down the tree trunk and in so doing could not see either turkey. Feeling very good and perhaps even a little proud I made my way to the turkey that was furthest away.

As I came upon the scene where the turkey fell I found all manner of feathers, a small pile of grain some skin and a little blood and a lot of feathers. On examination I determined that I had hit the turkey directly in the craw and it had lost the grain it held therein. It had also lost the function of the craw and consequently, in time, its life, but the fatally wounded turkey was no where in sight. I searched and searched only to find nothing. Giving up on that one I decided that only one turkey was to be my bag that day so I made my way over to the second turkey to pick it up. This time I found only feathers. No turkey, grain or skin or even blood could be seen. So in the course of some 45 minutes I had harvested only feathers off two very fine fowl that would be meat for the coyotes that night. Some hunt turkey only with shotguns and would say to me to use one instead of my rifle. In answer I tell you that I have used shotguns and can tell you the same kind of stories of losing turkey with this method also. Turkey, I decided, are not sure meat in the pot even when they appear very dead. In other words, "Don't count your turkeys until they are in the freezer."

Missing a Turkey up Close

Neck shots are hard to make even when turkeys are very close to you. One day mid-morning I heard a noise right next to my stand. On the alert I peered out to discover three large gobblers immediately in front of me at no more than seven yards. I carefully placed my rifle barrel out the front window and took careful aim on the largest turkey's neck. My problem was what part of the neck do I shoot? Up close to the head or down close to the body. For some reason that I cannot explain I chose the latter. A turkey's neck is, of course, covered with a lot of feathers. At the neck's junction with the body the feathers may be as much as six to eight inches in diameter while the neck itself is more like 1-1/2" in diameter. Given this fact one then has to decide just where in the six to eight inches of feathers is that 1-1/2" neck going to be? Well the answer is it moves around.

Not to be deterred I decided where to fire and fired. The turkeys decided to fly away; all of them. I guess my odds on hitting the turkey's neck were far better than the chances one takes when buying a lottery ticket but like 99.999999% of lottery ticket buyers I missed too.

All the turkeys I have taken; about 50% of those I have shot at were hit in the neck less than 4 inches from the head. I have never killed a turkey with a shotgun though I have shot at a few and have always missed.

Dusk as Shadows Fall

Significant in the deer hunter's planning is each day's end. Each hunter must answer the question of "What time in the afternoon do I go back to the deer stand?" For you see, all but the most devoted and intense deer hunters come back to the deer camp after the morning hunt, for lunch and a short afternoon nap. Feeder timers are set to feed at various times during the day, but mostly hunters time them to feed just after dawn and then about two to three hours prior to dusk. So the hunter must arrange to be in the hunting position at least an hour before the feeder is scheduled to feed in the afternoon. For you see a regularly timed feeding becomes part of the Doe family's daily schedule. Consequently

Mother Doe and her family will often arrive a few minutes before the set feeder time. So the wise and careful hunter arrives on the scene and conceals self at least an hour before. With hunter all settled in place, the area alarmed by the arriving hunter drifts back to a quiet woodland scene. Wildlife returns to the normal routine. Concealed the hunter must maintain absolute quiet and remain motionless if visible to the deer. Any noise or strange odor will disturb the hunted game.

Every hunter knows that the really large trophy bucks loath the light of day and just as much loath the feeder area. But due to doe in estrus they are uncontrollably drawn to where doe congregate. But even so a wary old buck will hang back in the cover until the light has deteriorated to almost dark before they will venture into the immediate feeder area. As the hunter waits patiently per chance a large buck is sighted in the fringe of the feeder area. The glimpses of him are not sufficient to provide a clear view or opportunity to shoot.

With heart thumping loud enough to be heard by the deer the wait goes on. Will he emerge before it is too dark to see? Will the hunter get a shot while there is enough light to clearly determine horn size? More often than not by a large margin the hunter gets no such shot. Big deer are big because they are cautious! Sometimes if the buck is not too careful he will approach the doe while it is still light enough to see. If out of the urgency of nature he makes this mistake it often will be his last.

Dusk: As Dark Sets In

Late evening in the Blue Mountains is a time of great serenity and beauty, as nature makes ready for starlight. The hunter once again knowing the deer feed late in the day will be in hunting position some two hours before sundown. Then the warm of the sun fades as it slowly sinks behind the terrain and the blue sky darkens from the east the deer families arrive to get in one last bite of food before darkness comes. Per chance it is a moonless night the deer will feed right up until it is almost too dark to see before they make their way off to their bedding place. But if there is a moon to take over the lighting responsibilities of the night the deer are not so given to leaving until all the available grain is consumed. Any feeding birds will have gone to their roost including the turkeys well before dark.

Dark Night and Imagination

If one is not accustomed to the great outdoors it is at this time of day that one can feel a bit isolated from what we call civilization. For the city dweller it can get very lonely after dark in the big ranch country. One can imagine all kinds of encounters with wild animals as one makes their way back to their vehicle. There is of course the problem of bucks in the rut. They have been known to attack man and in some cases kill humans with their horns and hoofs. Also there are the large cats, both Mountain Lions and Bobcats, and the wild hogs. Mother Hogs are somewhat like Bear when they have young ones with them and they can be somewhat unpredictable. And not to be ignored if the day has been a little on the warm side is the occasional rattlesnake coming out of the winter lair. The fertile imagination uses these possibilities to build in a small amount of anxiety.

So if a strange noise happens along the trail and your imagination has been active then one can get a rather large shot of adrenaline to cope with. And if this is a day when a hunting companion is picking you up, you walk to the appointed meeting place and wait. And wait. Long after you think your companion should have arrived you see the welcome glow of a distant headlamp from one of those marvels of the industrial age, a motorized vehicle. Most often it is a "pickup truck." If it is very cold and the wind is blowing such a glow is a very welcome sight for you know once inside you can begin to warm up a bit.

Recounting the Day's Hunt

Arriving back in camp after the evening hunt is always a highlight of the day. On everyone's mind is the question of whom got a kill that day and just how big was the unlucky buck. As the pickup gets to the last gate you can see that the light is on over at the skinning rack. Someone was successful. One might think such a moment brings jealousy or envy but such is not so. One always finds a warm welcome and good cheer when luck comes your way and it is you bringing in the kill. All rush out to the cleaning rack to check out the animal, its antlers and to witness in general. After spending a few minutes most will saunter back to the warmth of the eating shack and continue to swap hunting stories with the group. If it is one of those very cold north winds blowing you find yourself alone pretty quickly for usually the onlookers come out without coats or proper attire. If you need any kind of assistance to prepare your kill for the game cooler, someone will always get their warm cloths and assist without being asked.

In the camp house supper is being prepared by the volunteer of the day while each one asks the other the evening's key question. "See any deer?" If no, then on to someone who did see some at their stand. And then all in the group listen attentively as the "see'er" puts any drama that occurred into the story of his deer sightings. Including such interesting things as interactions between the deer. An interesting scene to watch is two mature bucks fight with their horns; hooking, slashing and generally pushing with all their might, the other. On these occasions one of the two will dominate and the other will flee. Bucks at times during these fights will actually penetrate the skin of their opponents with the sharply pointed tines of their antlers. Eyes are lost along with antler damage, which is fairly common. On occasion the fighting buck's horns will become so entangled that they become "locked." No amount of high velocity movement on the part of either or both bucks will serve to dislodge the entangled antlers. So on these occasions, it is usually the case that both buck die of exhaustion. But, some have reported seeing very large bucks in the field with just the head and some skin of the opponent buck hanging from the winner's antlers. It is a very strange sight indeed. Having the rotting flesh of your opponent hanging from atop your head is not in my mind a great way to celebrate success in battle.

So the day ends with all sharing the adventures of the hunt with companions over a home cooked meal though it be in a deer camp. Often it is a home cooked meal brought from home and prepared finally at the camp. These are always great meals and ones to remember in the years to come. Any deer hunter has a complete portfolio of meal stories to tell if only an interested audience was present. But meal stories are not the general fodder for deer camp conversation but rather all enjoy hearing from the storyteller how the "big one" got away.

Jeeps, Pickups and Other Special Transportation

Getting around the deer lease, from camp to stand, from stand to camp, filling feeders, fetching the kill all requires some type of rock climbing conveyance. And to fill this need there are plenty of answers. Help from those who have a new or old four-wheel drive vehicle is always appreciated.

Andy, one of my hunting pals and I decided we must go together and buy us an old jeep. This we soon accomplished complete with a tow-bar so we could tow it out to the lease. It turns out that our jeep has had more than a few mechanical deficiencies. First the carburetor was not connected correctly, had no automatic choke and was without a manual choke. After routine visits to the mechanic both in Mason and in Houston we still do not have it operating satisfactorily. While our jeep is always operating during the deer season it seldom is operating during the off season. It has been a help and in some ways a hindrance, at least to me.

Hindrance from a Jeep

The first year Andy and I had the jeep all my familiarity with jeeps got me in a bit of trouble early one morning. Well before sunup, I departed camp alone to go to my stand. There are two metal gates to go through to get to the pasture I was hunting in. When you are alone in the jeep you stop at the first gate, kill the engine, leave the jeep in low gear, exit the vehicle, walk up to the gate, open the gate, return to the jeep, get in, start the engine, shift into gear and drive through the gate. Once you are through the gate you stop the jeep, kill the engine, shift the jeep into low gear to keep it from rolling back or forward. Get out, walk back to the gate and close and secure it, walk back to the jeep, get in, start the engine, place the transmission in gear and proceed to the next gate to repeat the process. It was at this second gate that jeep familiarity got me into a heap of trouble.

I had opened the gate and driven through it using the procedure described above. On stopping the jeep, I placed it in gear preparatory to exiting when in fact I failed to get it securely into gear. This I determined when I stepped out and the jeep began to roll back toward the open gate. I quickly reached in and shifted it into gear to stop it and as I proceeded to close the gate I discovered that the jeep had rolled back enough so that the gate was in contact with the rear of the jeep when I closed it. Knowing that when I pressed in the clutch to start the jeep that it would likely roll back into the gate I hesitated. Then, I thought, this is no problem. I will simply start the jeep in gear (as I had done many times before with other old jeeps) and depart the gate in fine fashion without ever backing into it. For as I engaged the starter with the jeep in gear the engine would start with a lurch away from the gate leaving it safely behind.

I proceeded to get in the jeep, and immediately engaged the starter and sure enough the jeep started with a lurch, but to my amazement the jeep was in reverse. The gate suffered accordingly, as did the jeep. Just how did this happen to an accomplished jeep driver? Thinking through my procedure that morning it became apparent what had happened. As the jeep had rolled back I had placed it reverse to stop it from rolling into the gate. And left it in reverse rather than in low as I normally did and had forgotten this fact to my utter chagrin. Well the jeep engine did die before the gate was completely wiped out. It was however badly bent with latch chain broken and as you would guess both tail- lights of the jeep were broken and were hanging off the rear in plastic shreds. I was mortally embarrassed but not to be denied the hunt, I closed the gate and proceeded on my way. Later with some help from Roy, one of our hunters, we removed the gate, made of one-inch pipe, and laid it flat and stood on it to bend it back into a straight position. Remounting the gate and replacing the chain that had also broken completed the saga. Except for the jeep taillights that I replaced some months later with the help of Carrol, another fellow hunter at the lease.

A Jeep Tire Needs Air

When this event occurred I was driving a 1989 Chevy Suburban to and from the lease. It had some 150,000 miles on it and I had just recently had it all cleaned up, dings removed, rear bumper replaced and it was generally in fine condition and looked very good. In short I was happy with my "Sub" and was planning on driving it another 50,000 miles. As an accessory I always carry a battery-operated air pump with me. Noticing the left front jeep tire was low I thought of my air pump. And realizing I needed to start and run the jeep engine while I was at the lease anyway I decided I would start it and drive it over to the Sub. Once there I would get my air pump and air up the low tire.

The jeep started fine. I backed it out of its parking place, shifted into low gear and made the circle over to where I had the Sub parked. I decided I would pull up to the sub so the left front tire of the jeep was just at the left front door of the Sub so I could use the Sub lighter plug to do the air work. The jeep lighter plug was not working. This puts me driving directly toward the left side of the Sub. As I got near, I pressed the brake on the jeep and the brake pedal went all the way to the floor. It happened so suddenly and I was so close that I had no chance to recover. The jeep was moving slowly but with momentum, and proceeded to ram the left side of the Sub making several significant dings in the left rear panel. Needless to say I was not a happy camper. I did nothing else but put the jeep in reverse and drive it back to where it was before I took on this industrious notion and parked it.

"The tire can just go flat for all I care," I say's to myself. The jeep was surely a hindrance that day.

But the jeep has been a joy also. A stick shift jeep is a wonderful vehicle to learn to drive in. On a trip to the deer lease my wife and I took along our three granddaughters, Katie, Keren and Christina. The then thirteen-year old Christina had just about conquered the vagaries of driving the old jeep on our last visit. She was an apt student. I put her through all the paces in a dry run, shifting, clutching, accelerating and stopping. And I warned her that on the first few tries with the clutch she would find the jeep operating in great lurches and lunges as she learned the fine points of clutching. With her two sisters loaded in the back, not knowing what to expect but game enough to ride along, Christina made her first try. It was a giant lurch and all heads snapped as the jeep careened out of control. Christina was so surprised that she totally forgot what the process was to be. I yelled stop! Dutifully she stepped on the brake and succeeded in bringing us to a sudden neck-snapping stop. This of course set she and her sisters into waves of laughter. We tried it again and again until she had the starting and stopping accomplished. All we had to do was watch out for the few small shrubs and bushes in the area so we would not demolish them or damage the jeep. These driving lessons progressed to where I was willing that she try it solo, but to her disappointment the jeep took on a contrary notion and would not start. Back to the shop it went for another round of analysis and repair.

When Fellow Hunters Become Angels of Mercy

It was "supper time" in the cook shack one December. It was after dark. There was a light on and off drizzling rain. In the shack there was W.E., James, Jackie, Bill and I. The camp is well equipped with facilities. Along with a piped in water supply we have electricity, gas space heaters, two refrigerators, a microwave oven, a gas stove with oven, a separate food freezer and a walk-in cooler for the deer we kill. And to top the hunting camp luxury list, a regular bathroom, with commode and shower. Bill and I were eating leftovers, the rest were preparing various food items. For W.E., Jackie and himself, James was trying to bake in the microwave five or six nice Irish Potatoes for the three of them. Well this particular evening the Microwave was acting up. James "nuked" them for about 20 minutes and found they weren't even warm. James' back was giving him a lot of pain and he was a bit frustrated with the non-progress he was making with supper.

Recognizing his plight, I volunteered to take two of the potatoes over to our camper trailer and cook them in our smallish microwave. James agreed, so I took a plastic plate to cook the potatoes in and two large potatoes and made my way in the dark over to our trailer, a distance of about 40 yards. I set our microwave oven at max power for 10 minutes and stood there and waited while the potatoes cooked. On removing them they were too hot to hold so I placed them in a small piece of Tupperware to carry. With the potatoes in my left hand I stepped to the trailer door and stepped down the 12 inches to the steel trailer step. As I placed my foot on the wet trailer step and shifted my weight my foot slipped and down I went quick as a blink. My lower back hit the trailer step on the way down and my foot landed on the wooden step below, only to slip again and further down I went with my lower back taking a beating. It was over before I could utter a word. I landed bottom first with my lower back again taking the brunt of the blow on the outer edge of the wooden step.

It hurt. I mean it hurt a lot! Amazingly I was still holding the Tupperware with the potatoes and they had not spilled. Moaning loudly I forced myself to roll over and get up. It did not feel as though I had broken any bones. I walked over toward the cook shack groaning loudly with pain every step. By the time I got to the shack I was able to enter silently and tell them I had just take a bad fall and injured by lower back.

Bill, being a DDS, immediately got a plastic sack ice pack together and gave it to me to place on my back. This I did and sat down in a chair and held the ice pack in place for the next hour as we discussed what to do. We discussed my potential injuries and several of the guys said that if I had a broken pelvis I would not have been able to walk at all. So in their opinion that was not one of the possibilities. I tended to agree for I was at least able to get around at that time. The pain had subsided to a tolerable level so I decided to opt to spend the night and if not better by morning to go to a doctor or emergency room for some x-rays the next day.

I was able to get up and walk fairly comfortably over to our trailer where I went to bed with my clothes on. And I found that if I lay on my left side and kept very still I could rest comfortably. James was very concerned being our Lease Manager so he brought over some strong pain tablets his doctor had given him for his back pain. I had a liter of water and took the first of the two tablets. In about 30 minutes I was resting comfortably. Since the other two tablets would not last me the night James left me with two tablets that had different painkiller in them. I drank plenty of water and relieved myself in a homemade urinal. Bill, a great friend, dutifully dispensed with this waste when the container filled. I took the second round pain tablet about midnight. By 4:00am I was again in much pain so I took one of the other "backup" tablets.

Something in the latter tablet made me nauseated. When I am in such a condition I do not feel like moving at all. So when day came I simply could not move for the nausea and for reasons of pain. I tried to stand for a just minute and the pain was so intense in my lower back that I went into a mild state of shock. Reclining again the pain subsided but I was unable to move from my left side. Anytime I made the slightest effort to move the pain was so intense that I would cry out. Loudly! One time I sneezed. The pain was so intense I prayed out loud to God to "Please do not allow me to sneeze again." He answered this prayer. For normally I sneeze in twos. The second sneeze never came. I have had some intense pain in my lifetime with kidney stones and that sort of pain and this was more intense than that. A sharp, penetrating pain that radiated out from my bruised back like multiple lightning bolts racked my body anytime I chose to move my hip.

I told the guys to just plan on leaving me be that day and we would create a plan to move me the next day to San Antonio or Houston to an emergency room. Bill prepared me food for breakfast, lunch and dinner and kept me supplied with water and waste disposal services and all the other guys stopped in several times during the day to check on my progress.

We did create a plan for my evacuation the next morning. At the camp someone, years before, had left a stretcher. It was substantial and in good condition. Since I could not even stand to move we determined that if we worked it just right the guys could get me on the stretcher and carefully move me out of the trailer into the back of my Suburban onto a sponge rubber mattress. Bill worked throughout the day preparing everything for the next morning. He prepped the Suburban bed. He and the guys brought in the stretcher and made a dry run on the moves and mechanics of getting me onto the stretcher, out of the trailer and into the Suburban.

The back pain was by then centered in an area about the size of my hand high on my right buttocks just over the right "SI Joint." Pain spasms occurred throughout the night and I slept fitfully and found on a number of occasions I would awaken in pain and would be rubbing the SI Joint area vigorously to break up the spasms. I drank lots of water and Bill disposed. Before daybreak the next morning all were there to execute the plan. These fellow hunters were Angels in disguise. They worked that stretcher in such a way that I literally had not one pain attack as they moved me. After a few hard fought minutes in tight quarters they had me out of the trailer and deposited in the back of my Suburban on the foam pad and in Bill's very fine sleeping bag of nylon, rayon etc.

Bill drove and the others went along through the seven gates to the highway to make our trip a little more expeditious. We were on the way to Houston by 7:00am. As soon as the cell phone could get adequate signal strength I called my wife Ginny and told her of my condition and plans. She said she would meet me at the emergency room when I arrived to assist checking me in. The ride was not a bother to my back since I was very comfortably established in the back of the suburban. Around 9:00am I began to make calls to my Orthopedic Physician. Getting his office on my cell phone I told them of my condition and I would be in Houston at the Diagnostic Hospital emergency room by 11:30am. I then called the Emergency Room and informed them I had taken a fall at the deer lease and informed them of my arrangement with my doctor.

Bill did a masterful job of driving and we were indeed at the emergency room right at 11:30am. The Diagnostic Emergency Room apparently treats a lot of these "deer lease falls" and expected a broken spine or hip. The nurses and attendants were expecting me and had a gurney ready and in just a few pain-free minutes I was very professionally established in the emergency room and on my way into x-ray. The doctor was in surgery and as soon as he was free I gave him a rundown on what had happened. The x-ray revealed no bones broken so off to the MRI machine I went to make sure. This modern device failed to find a broken bone with its high-tech probing eyes so I was declared free of broken bones. Throughout all the gurney traveling I did, and time I spent in the x-ray and MRI, I remained in Bill's sleeping bag. Until they ruled out a broken bone they allowed me to keep it and I can say it kept me warm in those cold rooms. The Interns and Residents all and singularly debriefed me and gave me insight into the likely cause of my intense pain. It seems when such a fall happens and deep contusions occur the injured muscle sends a "don't use me, I'm in the repair mode" message to the brain in a series of lightening like bolts of pain. These are so intense that they do indeed suffice to cause one to lie uncommonly still so these injured muscles can heal.

My Physician said I would remain in the hospital that night and go home the morrow. And that he would send the therapist in to teach me how to walk with all the pain. This he did and indeed by the end of the day and through a lot of loud outcries from the pain I was able to navigate comfortably without outcry albeit slowly with a walker. The next day, with my wife's loving aid I did arrive home. Recovery took about two weeks before I could lie in any position other than on my left side.

Through this painful experience I came to appreciate the close companionship of those who hunt the Blue Mountains with me and served as my angels of mercy that December morning in 1997 when they carefully loaded me from trailer into Suburban with no pain. No small feat and to them I shall forever remain grateful. And grateful for a caring and loving wife who understands a deer hunter husband's fondness for the outdoors and all the experiences, both good and painful that come from the process of hunting deer.

A MISSISSIPPI HUNT AND A DOG

A Plantation Hunt

A Deer Dog

On this hunt I was a guest of a friend whose family and a few friends hunted a very old plantation property in Southern Mississippi near but not on the river proper. In the early 1800's the place was a large cotton plantation but the affect of time and nature had resulted in a natural re-forestation process. There was little evidence there had ever been a single agricultural crop grown on the place for the year we hunted there it was a mature woodland.

On natural re-forestation the following will illustrate my point. The Natches Trace lies Southwesterly to Northeasterly through Mississippi. Remaining to this day are many places where one can pay a visit to the old roadway itself. I have done so and find there in the deep forest a distinct roadbed depression in the soil long distances across the woodland. A depression in the soil worn by thousands of wagons and other equestrian traffic passing that way before and after the Civil War. On inspection one will typically find giant trees growing in the old roadway. Seeing such brings back the realization that while trees take decades to grow, 15 decades is plenty of time for several trees to come and go in the natural procession of things. Left alone forests' do recover from man's interventions.

Our hunting mode was with the use of highly trained hounds. Each morning a plan would be devised for the placement of hunters aligned along a natural or manmade landmark such as a logging road. One of the hunters would take the dogs, usually about three and lead them into the woods distant from but towards the now aligned hunters. The hoped for end result was that the dogs would "jump" a deer and that the deer would make his path of escape in such a way that would bring the deer within shooting distance of one the stationed hunters.

I was in such a position just prior to the break of day. Dawn came easy like with the sun's rays giving promise of another beautiful autumn day. Off to the North I can hear the distant barking and of dogs in the chase. I was standing right in a distinct game trail along which deer moved every day. The dogs seemed to be coming in my direction and I increased my alertness for a deer will be several hundred yards ahead of a dog early in the chase. I waited. Soon coming down the trail was a lone doe of about two to three years of age.

She was coming right towards me. At about 10 yards distance she suddenly stopped for she saw me in the middle of her path. Motionless standing there I saw her then turn around 180 degrees and retreat on the exact path she came on. After about one hundred yards she went to her right out into the woodland. Her appearance and retreat took no more than 45 seconds. About two minutes later a 30-pound Beagle appears giving chase and barking with a slow but consistent rhythm. The Beagle approached me in the same path trailing the doe by scent. When the Beagle reached the place the deer had stopped the Beagle stopped. At this point the Beagle was a bit puzzled but immediately set to work to "sniff out" the situation. The dog checked the trail ahead right up to where I was standing, then went around me giving no indication that I was even there and made a large circle back to the point the deer stopped. The Beagle then did another amazing bit of detective work with its nose.

Facing me on the trail the Beagle cut to my left exactly perpendicular to the trail for about 10 yards. Then turned right and made a quarter circle back to the trail. Finding no scent in that direction the Beagle came down the trail again to where the doe stopped. This time the beagle cut to my right, again exactly perpendicular to the trail for the prescribed 10 yards. Then turned left and again made a quarter circle back to the trail. Satisfied that the deer had not escaped by some gigantic leap to the right or left the Beagle, without delay wheeled about and gave chase back down the trail it had come on and turned off at the exact point the deer left the trail three minutes before. With this exhibition of trail wisdom I at once was impressed and even amazed at the methodology of the hound and have had a generous appreciation for the intelligence of hunting dogs since that date.

AN ILLINOIS BASSET AND A DEER

Chuck

The Chase

Our family once owned a Basset Hound named Chuck. Chuck loved to hunt, as did I, so on one occasion I took him out to a place where I hunted deer to see if we could locate some birds or rabbit. Chuck had a fine nose for odor. His nose was quiet long and I suppose filled with olfactory gland from end to end. In fact, his scenting ability was so fine he could smell things that other dogs didn't seem to scent. As a consequence he was a very slow hunter, preferring to sniff up each blade of grass or twig where game had been. A great deal of patience was required to hunt with Chuck.

On this trip he was slowly making his way through the brush when, suddenly a deer jumped up from its bed and bounded away. Slowness left Chuck in that instant. Chuck took off right on the deer's trail. As he ran I yelled "Come back, Chuck come here, all in vain. With his short legs I was certain he was going to damage his undercarriage in all the brush he was leaping over. Away into the woods they went, deeper and deeper as his bark grew fainter and fainter. At last I could hear Chuck no longer, "Gone out of hearin'" is what they called it in the old days. I waited until I was afraid I would have to go home without him but decided to wait another hour for him to return. Frequently I interspersed a whistle in the waiting to let him know where his starting point was. About 45 minutes later he "drug" himself back to the starting place a very tired and happy Basset hound. His tongue was out and as long as his ears and wonder of wonders, his under-carriage looked undamaged.

ROCKY MOUNTAIN HUNTS

Piceance Basin in 1953

One of Seven

As a young engineer just out of college an invitation to hunt mule deer in Colorado's Piceance Basin brings me sheer excitement. The year was 1953. Jack Englishby, a coworker, wife Lynn, two Po brothers and their wives and me, an unmarried single male for an exciting and enjoyable trip to Rio Blanco, Colorado and beyond. The youngest Po brother was just married and this hunting trip was to be he and his new brides' honeymoon. We loaded my new 1952 Chevy two door hardtop and the eldest Po brother's pickup with all our camping gear and drove to Colorado. Stopping for only gasoline and food we made it in about 28 hours to the ranch we were to hunt arriving late in the day.

After dinner at the ranch house with our host we took a night time spotlighted deer viewing tour of the lower pastures and saw hundreds of mule deer grazing in the meadows. Migration from the high range to the low range was in full swing. Our timing was perfect for a great hunt. The first night there we all slept at the ranch. The next morning we drove 20 miles southwest and uphill from the ranch house to our camping spot.

We were using a 12' x 12' wall tent for housing. Along the back wall we placed our air mattresses and sleeping bags side by side with the foot of our mass bedding facing the tent entrance. How do three married couples accommodate an unmarried single guy in their bedded midst? My colleagues had this all planned out. The arrangement was this wise, from left to right looking in from the tent door. On the far left, the new bride; next to her of course her new husband, then the single me. Next to me my friend Jack then his wife, then the other Po brother's wife then her husband. So it was female, male, male, male, female, female and male. How's that for keeping a single guy out of harms' way? This was no problem for me but the question I have is "How would you like to spend the first seven nights of your honeymoon sleeping with five other people in a 12' x 12' tent?" Hunting does have its priorities I admit but this one takes the prize I believe.

Other hunters were not far away in the ranch back country Cow Camp. A combination bunkhouse and kitchen situated on the shore of a small lake. We went for a visit the first evening and found a general alcohol excessive consumption problem when we arrived. Several were more than a bit intoxicated and poor judgement was prevalent it seemed to me. One of the hunters who was the ranch owner who lived out of state had a new pistol which all were admiring. Several of us took turns firing the pistol out the back door at targets across the lake.

When we had finished, the pistol's owner decided he would target practice inside the camp house itself. Spying an empty whiskey bottle on a kitchen cabinet he took aim and fired, breaking the bottle into a thousand pieces which scattered all over the kitchen. The unspent bullet continued on its way penetrating the log wall of the kitchen. Without further ado we excused ourselves and went back to camp and solitude. Our camp was without "alcoholic beverage" as was our predilection when hunting.

Late that night the shouting and laughing of the drunken Camp-house hunters wakened us. They were out in front of our tent having a good time. They departed and we slept until the next morning when we found the subject of their laughter. They had killed a large doe and left it in front of our tent. The next day Jack and one of the Po brothers delivered the doe back to them at the Camp-house. Sober minds prevailed and they used her for camp meat.

The second night there was a good six-inch snow that provided a tremendous advantage for us. First it quelled the dust; for some weeks prior to our arrival it had been very dry and the Rocky Mountains were in a fire watch mode. Second it provided excellent tracking and sighting of animals for they would be easy to see on the white background of the snow.

Without Alcohol

The term "without alcoholic beverage" leads to a funny story occurring later in the week. We had been hunting for several days and had a few animals for our trouble. It was our plan to take home at least one mule deer for each one in our party which numbered seven. On this day the ladies all remained in camp while the men left early on the hunt. On returning to camp we found two of the ladies sick at their stomachs from what we concluded was altitude sickness. Jack later received the true story for Lynn, his wife.

Seems the girls were all a-giggle over a bottle of wine they had found in the trunk of my car. Two of them sampled it and found it of poor taste and put it back not knowing what the liquid was. The wine bottle they found was nothing but pure anti-freeze for my radiator. Its attractiveness was from its very pretty color it seems. This anti-freeze-wine-decoy came on the scene in the following manner. When preparing for the trip I had drained my radiator and had added pure antifreeze for the trip. Having some left over I scrounged around my apartment for something to save it in and found an empty wine bottle. You know the rest of the story!

Missed the 36 Inch Spread

On the second day of our hunt about mid-morning I walked over a small knoll up in the mountains and sighted a number of deer bedded down on a snow covered ridge I estimated at some 400 yards distance. I immediately lay down in the snow and glassed the herd. Right in the center was the largest mule deer buck I had ever seen. He was huge and his rack was huge. I estimated at least 36 inches in spread. In a prone position with excellent rest I planned my shot. The buck was bedded and not in a good position for a shot so I determined to wait on the off chance he would get up soon. As deer are apt to do, one of the herd had spotted me and began a leisurely appearing plan of withdrawal. My target joined in and rose to standing and perfectly broadside to me. Great sight-picture, squeeze it off, "boom" and my buck and the herd rapidly departed the bedding area. I was astounded. How could I miss? Making my way over to the area I did find just a tad of hair and a little sliver of skin right where my target had been standing. I tracked for about a mile to no avail. On examination the range had been longer than my estimated 400 yards and I had undershot my target getting just a piece of brisket. A chance of a lifetime it turned out.

The Eleven Shot Sunrise Buck

I have never fired as many times at a single deer as I did on this trip. The situation in the hunt was we were walking along brushy draws, casting stones into them to frighten out any deer holed up there. On this occasion just as the sun was peaking over the far ridge to the east a nice antlered buck jumped up and began an assent of that far ridge. I was in position to get the shot, so with my "sporterized" military Enfield, six round magazine deer rifle, I began my effort.

The range was long but I was not unprepared for I had carefully sighted in my weapon at distances up to 500 yards prior to leaving home. Taking my time, shooting off-hand but aiming carefully through my six-power scope with the rising sun glaring in the objective lens I shot and shot and shot. The deer continued undeterred on its way to the top of the ridge. After the seven shots that emptied my gun the buck reached the top of the ridge and began to run along the ridge to my right. For the next four rounds, each loaded in single-shot fashion, I continued my effort to bag this bounding mule deer buck. Just as I fired my eleventh round the buck made its way over the ridge and out of sight seemingly unharmed. I was downcast and discouraged but my companions assured me that a running deer was no cinch to hit especially at the distances I was firing. But we decided in good sportsmen's like manner we really should take a look over the ridge where the deer was last seen on the off chance it had been hit.

Crossing the draw we made our way to the spot and walked along looking for blood but found none. A little further we did find a very dead buck. And believe it or not it had only one bullet hole in the lung cavity. One of the last four shots had indeed found the target. This converted a defeated feeling to one of thanksgiving for my first mule deer buck was a good five by five.

Crack, Bomp, Sissle, Boom and the Laws of Physics

Most people have never been shot at, hence are not aware that the sounds from a deer rifle are very different when the gun is fired in your direction. My acquaintance with "Crack, Bomp, Sissle, Boom" came on this hunt to the Piceance Basin. Jack and I were walking a draw on opposite ridges. Jack was a fine shot with his favorite .270 Winchester and had shot at extreme distances as well. On this very cold, windless morning Jack and I could actually converse in only slightly elevated voices though some 600 yards separated us. Jack tells me that he has sighted a nice buck and intends to shoot. I could not see the deer so I got down behind a rock for cover and what I heard was really something quite different than I expected.

First I heard a "crack", then I heard a "bomp", then a "sissle" then a "boom." On reflection I determined that the laws of physics did apply. The rifle bullet at about Mach four arrived first, the "crack" was the miniature sonic boom of the bullet arriving, then the bullet found its target nearby, the "bomp" as the animal was hit. After this I heard the "sissle" which was the bullet sound as it traveled through air, and then arriving last at Mach one on my ear-drum was the muzzle blast of Jack's .270 some 600 yards away. The deer had been only 400 yards from Jack so he got a clean kill.

To Meeker in 1954

The year after the first Piceance trip with Jack and gang, my friend Andy and I traveled to Colorado to hunt near Buford, Colorado on the White River just out of Meeker. We were anxious to get on with it so we departed Texas early arriving at the ranch three days before the season was to open. Dallas Collins, the ranch foreman and his family were our hosts. Andy and I were assigned a very nice bunkhouse for sleeping and we were to eat with the Collins family.

We became voluntary ranch hands for the ensuing three days as we helped bring in hay from the fields and store it for winter. Sure enough on the third day late in the afternoon it began to snow. We were more than glad to help and it felt good that we had made a contribution to the operation and were not simply getting a free ride.

The first morning of the season, well before dawn Andy and I made our way 1500 feet up the nearest mountain seeking the higher ground for a mule deer buck. Soon after daybreak we sighted a nice buck that Andy took with one well-placed shot. We field dressed it, covered it over with brush to keep the magpies off and continued our hunt.

At the rancher's place there was an old jeep that ran but had no brakes nor did the clutch work. Nevertheless we took it up the mountain to Andy's kill only to find a bear had beat us to the deer and had eaten away both hindquarters. And the jeep served us well later in the hunt.

For you see a jeep has a low gear in four wheel drive so low that it will brake the jeep itself, so all one has to do is to place the jeep in low-low gear and proceed to descend the mountain. It is very slow but there is just one hitch. Be sure it stays in low gear for there is no way you can get it back into low if it ever gets out. But being a jeep buff, I knew that a jeep could be driven without a clutch or brakes. All one has to do is place the jeep in low gear and press the starter and away you go. The engine starts in low gear and you are on your way. A jeep can even be shifted from low to a higher gear without a clutch. Here is all that is required to move out of the lower gear after you begin to roll. Reduce the engine speed just enough to cause a synchronization of the engine speed and the gear speed at the higher speed and easy like shift into the higher gear. If one hears a gear clatter then slow down the engine a tad more until the gears mesh and you are in the higher gear. Or if slowing the engine only increases the frequency of the clatter than you must go in the opposite direction by speeding up the engine to reach gear synchronization speed. This can be done with practice for I have done it many times. I am not saying this type operation is good for the gearboxes! But will work in a pinch when the clutch goes out on you in some far off place and you would like to ride back to camp rather than walk. On another day we did kill a nice buck far up the mountain but near a road. Again we called the old jeep into action and retrieved the deer without difficulty.

The Biggest Animal I Ever Saw

Dallas Collins was willing for us to give him the cow elk we were to kill so we set out one morning to find one. Andy and I walked up a mountain trail with a wide view of the surrounding area and stopped to glass when we saw a long single file of cow elk. There did not seem to be a bull in the bunch. We saw them approaching in single file when they were still at least a mile away and they were headed in our general direction. Andy and I took different positions of vantage and waited. As the lead cow came over the hill east of us and came within 100 yards of our positions I fired at her. Almost at the same instant I heard Andy fire also. "Oh no," I thought, we are going to get more cows than the one we want. But only the lead cow went down. We arrived at the carcass and on exchanging information we had both been shooting at the same cow. I had a large hunting knife that I left with Andy to do the gutting and went back to our initial spot to retrieve our miscellaneous gear. Expecting Andy to have made moderate progress while I was away I was somewhat surprised when I returned and found him walking around the carcass still in amazement.

"Andy," I asked, "Why haven't you started with the gutting?"

He replied, "That is the largest animal I have ever seen and I cannot get her positioned right."

Indeed it was a very large cow! So with coordination we moved her to a more promising position and began the cleaning. It took a little while for neither of us had ever had the challenge of cleaning such a large animal. We estimated her weight at five to six hundred pounds. By then it was late evening and we turned her over and departed for the ranch house. Again the next morning the old ranch jeep came in handy one more time. Dallas went along and helped us quarter her and get the quarters up into the jeep. Of course there were horses we could have used but they would be more trouble than one with gasoline for fuel. That evening, before our departure the next morning, we had a festive meal by Mrs. Collins of elk steak, biscuits and gravy along with a vegetable or two.

At the end of a great five-day hunt we were on our way back to Houston in Andy's new 1954 Olds with priceless memories and our two mule deer bucks in our trailer.

Piceance Again in 1974

Exactly 20 years later Ron Kingsbury, Phil Belanger and I took Phil's camper trailer on another excursion into the Piceance Basin. We were all living in the St. Louis area at the time. We departed St. Louis as an arctic cold front crossed the mid-west and we fought a modest amount of snow and ice all the way to Denver. As we traveled we talked of many things but I remember distinctly that one of our conversations was about how many rounds of ammo we each had brought. Phil and I had each brought several boxes but Ron steadfastly maintained that he had brought but one round. Saying that he intended to get his one deer with his one round. As far as we knew that was all he had and I do not know differently even until this day.

Slippin' and Slidin' in Denver

We arrived in the city of Denver early morning just at the break of day. As we made our way westward through the city we were suddenly on a long, four-lane overhead roadway that made a turn to the left and was therefore sloped to the left and as soon as we hit it we found it was covered with ice. Fortunately there was no oncoming traffic for as we proceeded westward the truck and camper began a slow migration from the far right side of the road into the adjoining lane then slowly into the oncoming lanes and over toward the left hand guard railings. There was literally nothing I could do except keep steering straight, no sudden turns please, no brakes for we were on black ice. Would the road width last until we cleared the overhead? Just as we were about to collide with the left railings we cleared the overhead and the ice. Our guardian angels were surely with us that morning for had there been oncoming traffic we would have been in a rather nasty collision ending our hunting trip in dramatic and drastic fashion. We stopped soon after and laced on the chains for we were in a section where ice and snow had begun to accumulate.

Snow Lightning

Sometime late in the day we made it to Rio Blanco and on to our hunting area in Piceance Basin on public land. Selecting our campsite we set up for the night. It was bitter cold. We put food in the ice chests to keep it from freezing solid. That night it snowed about four to six inches. Just enough to take down the dust and provide hunting visibility.

But what I remember most about that heavy snow was the electrical activity that came with it. We were in the midst of the most violent electrical lightning storm I had ever experienced. It was very scary, for laying there in that metal camping trailer with nothing but a tent over your head hearing all the thunderbolts and wondering just what the lightning was striking all the time. It was a continuous and unending bedlam as I remember it today. All this noise was occurring in the midst of a quietly falling snow. There was no wind, just thunderbolt after thunderbolt sounding as though the lightning was striking within yards of the trailer. There just wasn't much to be struck except the tops of the adjacent hills. But again we were not harmed. Ron must have been very calm that night for when we recall that hunt he cannot remember the lightning at all. Me I'll never forget for I was really scared.

Missing a Nice One Again

Well we all three climbed the adjoining 600' hill the next morning before daylight. It was a hard climb in the snow but we made it. We split up on top and I found a nice vantage-point next to a mountain roadway which we found on top. We later determined we actually could have driven to the spot. Blasé orange was required clothing and from position mid-morning I could see five hunters in addition to we three that were on the mountain. About noon I made another count and could see none. I imagined that since it was so cold and the hunting slow they had all retreated to their camps. That afternoon I spotted Ron down 200' below my elevation and 500 yards away, easing through the brush.

When he was closer I yelled at him and in so doing spooked a nice mule deer buck down on Ron's level that ran off to my left and away from Ron so I took careful aim and fired. Ron recalled later that the shot startled him as I knew it would but I had no time to warn him and he was in no danger for I was shooting away from his direction. I hit the deer but it did not deer but it did not fall. It was then and there, that I received another lesson in basic deer intelligence. I could see perhaps a mile down through the snow-covered terrain and somewhat timbered mountainside. But I never saw that buck after I shot. It seemed that it simply disappeared.

Thinking proudly that I had got him I descended to the spot where I had fired at him and found a little blood and a little hair and that was all. It seems my lesson in downhill shooting 20 years before had done me no good for the deer was wounded and was gone. From that point Ron and I tracked the deer for a mile. There were blood drops for a little way but that buck had put piece after piece of vegetation between my position and him. He had gotten down on his knees to go under low hanging branches on trees and taking the path he took and looking back at my vantage-point at no time was his tracks in sight from where I was. The buck, though wounded, had given me the slip. My guess is that I just grazed his back by not allowing for the downhill angle. Had the shot been just a tad lower it would have penetrated his spine and would have been fatal. We had no luck finding him and gave up very disappointed for he was a good-sized mule deer. That buck knew how to hide while traveling. I have heard of others who have actually seen bucks "knee walk" to stay out of view.

Ron and the One Shot Slay-ride Deer

We all liked the area so we were back the next day and Ron come upon a nice buck and (true to his promise) took him with a single shot from his rifle. The story is though, the deer was on the other side of the smallish mountain we were climbing to get to the hunting area so we determined that we could not pull him up to the top to the road so we planned an alternate route to recover Ron's deer. About a mile down the mountain away from camp there was an oil field road we could get to in Phil's pickup. So Ron determined that he would simply pull the deer the mile down the snow-covered slope to the road. Well that turned out to be a lot easier than we thought, for all Ron had to do was point the deer in that direction and he literally rode the deer down the mountain to the road. In so doing he would steer by dragging his feet. It wasn't terribly steep so he was in no danger of a runaway-deer-ride but it did make the task a bit easier that we thought. Perhaps even a little enjoyable for in a way it was a "deer-slay-ride." We picked Ron and the deer up at the appointed spot.

Sprayed by a Coke

One of the humorous things that happened to us on that trip happened the day we decided to have a can of coke. We had bought a six-pack of Coca Cola to refresh ourselves with, but they had frozen up pretty badly. So on a trip we placed the six-pack in the truck by the heater outlet to thaw a bit as we journeyed. Along the way we decided to open the cokes. Well we got quite a surprise when we did so. Ron was driving, I was in the middle and Phil was on my right. I took a can and opened it. The can was still under a lot of pressure from being frozen and thus immediately began to spray vigorously. I handed the spraying coke to Ron to open the window and point it outside. He forgot that he had rolled the window up and attempted to put the can through the glass.

This, while the can was spraying what looked like a gallon of sticky, sugary coke foam all over Phil's pickup cab. Phil was a great sport and we laughed until our sides hurt thinking of the silly scene we made trying to get the coke out the window. We were not going to have coke in the truck again. Of that we were sure.

"Packing In" in 1977

To Pagosa Springs

A few years later I joined a hunt with some friends in Houston to do a pack-in hunt in Southwestern Colorado. Jim, our lead hunter, was an Oklahoma native who had brothers in Oklahoma who ran cattle feed lots. He and his brothers were regular pack-in hunters to Colorado so he invited several of us to join them in a pack hunt. The brothers had access to all the pack animals; horses, burro and mules along with packing gear, and transportation needed. We used all three and lots of gear. Several of us set out from Houston to join Jim's brothers in Colorado. They were driving a 18-wheel cattle trailer with all that we would need, hunting gear, baggage, tent, pack gear, animals and feed for a five day hunt. I brought along a Morsan wall tent and cooking gear. In all there were 14 of us at the rendezvous point near Pagosa Springs.

Early morning saw us on our way. Some were riding and some were walking leading pack animals. I was in the latter group. Until late evening we walked. Running completely out of energy I had to stop along the way. The others went on and came back for me with an animal to ride on into camp. In an hour or so we were all set up in our camp and supper was cooked and eaten.

Notable in this hunt was the absolute lack of mule deer in our area. I did see a small heard of cow elk one day and that was it. We were in the wrong place for mule deer that was clear to us all. One of our group finally took one buck of medium size but in the main we were skunked. Why am I telling this story then? Well I especially wanted you to meet "Ethel" the errant pack burro.

Ethel the Burro

Ethel was a fairly young burro who had in fact been sent to Pack School by her owner, one of Jim's brothers. Ethel was at first very stubborn and then totally obdurate. No amount of coaxing would get Ethel to willingly accept a pack on her back. But our packing boss was also a stubborn man. It seemed that no amount of kidding from all could get him to give up on Ethel. So the pack trip in and out was a battle of wills between the pack boss and Ethel. In all the trouble he had with Ethel I never once heard him raise his voice or in other way speak disparagingly of Ethel. He was both determined and patient. He would work with Ethel it seemed to me endlessly to get her all rigged out with all her pack and gear on her back. It seemed it took more time to pack Ethel than all the other animals combined, some 10 of them.

On the way in it so happened I was assigned to lead Ethel. She was nice and cooperative. This was not too bad for me until Ethel got tired about mid-day and decided she had had enough of this. She simply stopped in the trail and would not budge a bit further. Well, I understood her plight for I was to be in the same predicament soon. And I knew I was certainly no match for Ethel so the pack boss took over and after about thirty minutes Ethel succeeded in bucking and in general resisting until all the gear on her back was under her stomach. Ethel was tied to a tree and unloaded and allowed to rest awhile. While tightly snubbed to the tree she was repacked. Then on untying her she immediately acted out the gyrations necessary to move the pack from her back to her stomach once again. In final desperation the pack boss allowed Ethel to win this round and put the pack on his riding horse and let Ethel trail along without a load the remainder of the way.

All through the five days we were camped Ethel was frequently the subject of conversation. Jokes became frequent about Ethel winning the battle of wills between her and the pack boss. All the while the pack boss was reassuring everyone that Ethel was a fine and valuable burro and not atypical of her breed. That Ethel would be fine on our return out to the tractor-trailer rig we had left beside the mountain road. Well this bit of prophecy was not all that accurate. For the morning of our planned departure Ethel once again was a time consuming challenge for the pack boss. With Ethel secured firmly to a nearby tree he placed Ethel's pack on her and cinched it down tightly. Once this was accomplished we set out on our all day journey out of the wilderness area. We were still within sight of the camp when Ethel began her now familiar gyrations. In a flash she had displaced her backpack and made it a stomach pack. Without fanfare the pack boss yielded to her whims and put her pack on his riding horse and allowed Ethel to trail along behind. When I think of determination I always think of Ethel.

"Packing In" in 1978

To Flattops

Not to be deterred the same group decided that the '78 hunt was so much fun that we would do it all over again in '79. The same process was used with duties as before and we all met in Carbondale, Colorado for our hunt in the "Flat-Tops Wilderness Area."

Ethel was once again with us and once again a challenge. But she did do noticeably more work than she had done the year before. That doesn't mean, however, she did this work willingly. The same approach and the same Ethel gyrations produced the same results but this time she would relent in her stubbornness when repacked the second time and carry her pack like a good little burro.

Again it was a full day's ride to the campsite. This time all 14 of us slept in a 15' x 30' wall tent. The weather became bitterly cold and all our food became solidly frozen. The potatoes were reduced when thawed to uncooked mashed potatoes, a soggy mess that we did not even try to recover. Notable among our culinary challenges during our camping in the Colorado high altitude deep freeze was managing our dozens of very frozen eggs.

We had a pot stove inside the tent where we kept a fire each night. Before bedding down we would peel the shells from about three-dozen frozen eggs and place the shell-less eggs in a container next to the stove so they would thaw during the night. This worked marvelously well but peeling frozen eggs, we discovered, will decimate your finger-tips leaving them raw and sore. Breakfast became our biggest meal with bacon-and-eggs, fry bread and milk gravy. We had managed to keep some of our food in the one ice chest and milk was one of those items. Somehow we managed to have decent food despite the sub-freezing temperature.

A Broken Rib Sends Me Home Early

After three days of, once again, a deer-less hunt we were getting discouraged. On the fourth day I was out on a walking hunt alone when in crossing an icy place I fell. I managed to catch myself somehow with my rifle by ramming it into the snow but in the fall the rifle butt impacted my rib cage. That night I could hardly breath without excruciating pain. Broken ribs were not new to me so I fashioned a rib belt out of a packing belt and tightened it around my rib cage. This gave me some relief and I could function at slow speed but still I was in some amount of pain. Several of us decided we would pack out early because of my injury. We did this the next day and arrived in Carbondale much relieved to be back where we could get warm. The rib had much improved so I deferred going for a x-ray until we got back to Houston. My first aid had done the trick for a separated rib-sternum cartilage.

Later Jim told us that his brothers had packed out the following day and in so doing had lost a packhorse down a steep embankment where we had to cross a narrow icy ridge top for about 100 yards. Wonder it wasn't Ethel but it wasn't. The horse and pack were recovered with some difficulty and they continued on their way.

Black Canyon of the Gunnison Country

Outfitter

In all my Colorado hunting I had not hunted with an outfitter so this was a new experience for me. Ron and I had preplanned this trip and were all set to fly to Grand Junction when a job requirement caused him to have to drop out. He passed his reservation to another hunting partner, Bill. It all worked just fine. Bill and I were met and driven to the ranch some two hours distance by the outfitter. Everything was all set for our mule deer hunt in an area with a nice elk herd. This was not the typical hunt for we were placed in various vantagepoints in a "glass the countryside" for deer approach. We in fact walked very little and I personally liked the approach a lot being a "flatlander." Particularly if the deer are on the move and it was the time of the year for that. However the mule deer were not on the move for we saw only four bucks in a five-day hunt. But we saw quite a number of elk. There were two experiences on this hunt I want to share with you.

Elk Antlers like Tree Branches at Dusk

One evening as I was walking in from a vantagepoint well after sundown I witnessed a most awesome and unforgettable scene. For all practical purposes it was dark except for a vivid scarlet glow in the western sky that was rapidly being overtaken by the dark shadows of night. As I walked over a small rise off to my left and to the west piercing the scarlet sky from the black of the shadows below were the antlers of five mature Bull Elk. The bulls were unperturbed by my presence, if indeed they could even see me for I was in dark clothing against a dark background and the slight wind was in my favor. I slowed as I eased gingerly on my way hungrily gathering in this breathtaking and unbelievable scene; elk antlers, only elk antlers. I could not see their heads only antlers, there silhouetted against the scarlet western sky. It was if the antler's them-selves were the branches of trees. The Bulls were unmoving, it seemed, that as one they all sensed my presence yet were fixed in alertness awaiting some noise, odor or other indication that they were in danger. A little concerned for my own safety in such close proximity to them, I tarried little as I eased by on my way to camp.

In the course of the ensuing years I have seen an occasional photograph of elk antlers silhouetted. And such always brings to mind a late evening in the Black Canyon of the Gunnison Country and a rare view of five sets of awesome elk antlers on display by the natural owners. Unforgettable!

A Long Shot

Every hunter can tell you of the time they made that long-distance rifle shot and connected. I have already told you of a couple instances where a long distance shot did not get the animal.

Placed at a vantage position well before dawn I waited in quiet solitude for a Colorado sunrise. It slowly came and impressive it was. As the mountainside became visible and the sparkling remains of scattered yellow Aspen leaves left a pleasing feeling in my eyes. I found myself attempting to glass a lot more territory than I could effectively cover. Nothing shows as the morning wears on. Around 10:00am two mule deer bucks appear over a small rise some 400 yards away. On this occasion the guide had alerted me about the "rise" and had given me the distance as he dropped me off that morning. He had said there was a water hole nearby and to keep my eyes open for game coming to water. Glassing the bucks I saw that one was a three by three and the other was a four by four.

My .270 was sighted in "dead-on" at 250 yards at sea level and I was hunting at around 9000 feet elevation. Shooting max-velocity with 130 grain Sierra Boat-tail bullets I had a very flat shooting load.

The outfitter had warned us that most all the missing his hunters had done over the years was in shooting over the animals. He cautioned, "Do not sight over your target." So against my better judgement I determined to hold right on the buck's shoulder and not allow for bullet drop. This I did with a solid rest and squeezed off a round. Both deer bolted and ran to my left as I faced them. As they sailed over brush I got off two more rounds before they disappeared. Hoping that at least one shot found its target I made my way to the spot where they had been standing and began a systematic search for any sign that I had hit one of them.

I found no indication at all that any of my shots were good. As I searched I kicked myself mentally again and again for not holding over the buck on that first shot. At least I told my self, I should have held high on his shoulder. I spent the next hour scouting for a dead deer or at least a spot of blood. I extended my search for several hundred yards to no avail. I crisscrossed the area three times to no avail. I finally determined it was not to be. At about 11:30am I was getting warm so I sought some shade and was standing near the spot where the deer were when I made the first shot, which was also near the ranch road. Waiting for my guide to pick me up I kept looking around the area while standing in the shade. The guide was obviously running late. About 30 minutes had passed when my eyes fixed on a rock not 20 yards from me that was of the same hue and color of a deer. Ever an optimist I walked toward the rock and as I came closer the rock looked more and more like the rump of a deer. Sure enough when I was quite close the rock indeed became a deer colored deer.

It was the four by four that by counting brow-tines was a nice five by five. The horns were not visible from my earlier shady viewpoint. As I gutted the buck I found that the rifle bullet had entered the deer's "rib-cage" at the exact spot I had aimed. So much for my doubt; the outfitter was right. Why, I wanted to know? The angle had been downhill at around 3 to 5 degrees. Not enough to affect the bullet very much. Could it be the elevation and thinner air that allowed the bullet to travel the distance without the sea level drop I was accustomed to? Right or wrong, I decided that was it. And my later research failed to bear my conclusion out so perhaps I was holding slightly higher than I thought; a most likely correct answer. Anyway I have the horns to prove I got'im.

THE CHEYENNE MOUNTAINS OF WYOMING

Mule Deer in Elk Country

The Skyline Buck

Out of Rock River, Wyoming one turns to the earth roads leading up and into the Cheyenne Mountains off to the Northeast. Some 40 miles later we are in the hunting camp of our outfitter, Ralph Abell of Laramie. The camp is nicely done sitting in a very picturesque area amid large granite like stones. Lodging and food are clearly a good value and the hunt area lies in a beautiful mix of plains and low-lying mountains. Hunting technique is a mix of driving to a prime location and getting on foot for a "looksee" at what game is in the area. A rather large elk herd is resident and drawing for a bull tag is slow and takes a few years on the average. This Mule Deer season there were extra tags available after the draw so I took one and joined Ron who had drawn a buck tag earlier.

A guide and I set off to scout out one of the prime areas. Driving into an area for an overview of a valley of grain fields below, the pickup sent a grazing buck into a run away and up the hill on the driver's side of the truck.

The guide immediately stopped the truck and exclaimed, "Look at that!"

"That" was easy to see for it was a mature, perhaps five year old, four by four buck. He stopped on the crest of the hill. Standing broadside with his head turned toward us he was a thing of marvelous beauty. Behind him the blue sky offered a photographer's dream shot but I had no camera. Gingerly opening the right door I eased out of the truck and viewed him with my 3x9 scope. As grand as he was he was not what I was looking for in a Mule Deer buck this trip. His antlers while high did not extend beyond his big mule ears. And that was a principal criterion for the buck I would take.

"Sky-lined" at about 50 yards and standing stark still I admired his beauty until he took to the "mule deer bounding run" on down the face of the mountain until he was out of sight.

The Grain Field Bucks

One of the several ranches we hunted had a large grain operation in one of the river deltas. We drove there several times looking for the size buck Ron and I wanted. In the western most area there were a number of huge 300 pound plus bucks. They were so large that when they walked they appeared ponderous as they sort of swayed side-to-side as they shifted their weight in the walk. On two occasions we jumped the larger of the group and watched him as he took a leisurely swaying lope over to the larger herd. There were four of the monsters in the bunch and we spent hours glassing them on several visits to the area hoping that at least one of them would show antlers noticeably wider than his ears.

While all the racks, four by four and five by five, were high and well balanced they just did not meet the measurements we were hoping to find.

On one occasion one of them was tending a doe some thirty yards from the ranch roadway and as we watched he became mildly alerted to our proximity and lumbered off. The grain field habitat was obviously great for body weight but did not provide the diet for large antlers.

While it was a great outing and we saw nice huge bucks we nonetheless went home without one. And that was fine with us for we were not meat hunting.

"Sufficient for the day is the joy of the hunt."

WESTCHESTER COUNTY, NEW YORK

An Apple Orchard Bow Hunt

Apple Pie

Why would I relate this story? Because if you love deer hunting and fresh "out of the oven" homemade apple pie then it will appeal to you and it isn't very long as a story goes. It happened back in 1965.

My friend Dan and I had been talking of taking our Long Bows on a whitetail deer hunt in Westchester County near where he and his family lived in Chappaqua, NY. It was on a very cold December morning that I made my way from New Jersey across the Tappan Zee Bridge to Westchester County, New York. Arriving well before dawn Dan joined me in the warm car and we drove to a place where he had arranged a permit for us to hunt. This was a buck or doe legal area so we were optimistic. The place was an operating apple farm of rather large proportion. Just as the sky was opening up with the light of day there was a heavy frost and the temperature was in the 20 degree F. range.

Our manner was one of still-hunting, yet slowly easing through the orchard that was a veritable forest with large apple trees with limbs almost touching the ground. Some of the limbs still had nice plump unharvested apples. We would ease from one row to the next peering down the openings for deer. The wind came up and we were getting very cold for we really did not expect it to be that frigid. After a few hours and no deer sighted, and with the wind chill plummeting we decided to get on home and warm up a bit for we were underdressed.

Here comes the good part. By the time we arrived back at Dan's home in Chappaqua we were famished for food as well. Incidentally, Chappaqua was the home of the 19th Century writer/publisher, Horace Greeley, who is remembered for advocating to those seeking fortunes. "Go west, young man, go west!"

On entering Dan's home my nose encountered the most delicious odor; one of those odors that cause one to recall pleasant memories of odors past and one that makes the saliva glands run like a faucet. What was it Sue was cooking? It turned out to be a wonderful "right-out-of-the-oven" homemade apple pie with the apples being from that same orchard we had been hunting. Now picture this. Dan and I are famished. Do we eat a sandwich first? Absolutely not! We sit down and with a cup of hot coffee we begin to devour that apple pie. In just a few minutes we had left Sue one medium sized piece and the rest went to create that zone of comfort in one's anatomy that comes when a very hungry hunter comes in from the field and is rewarded by something wonderful and quite unexpected. Mmmgood! Thanks again, Sue! I'll never forget that day and that pie.

You know, on reflection, deer hunting and the experiences that come along with it are to me a lot like homemade apple pie. They are good. They feel good. And they are good to remember also. Oh, once in a while one may get pie of rotten apples when trouble comes. But the good times far outweigh the bad.

I begin looking forward to the next deer season on the last day of the current one.

It is then we say, "Just think. It is only ten months until the deer season opens." Ten months to remember last year's hunt and all the hunts that went before. To remember all the friends you have hunted with and the fun times in the field together. Soon ten months become nine and sooner than you would expect you are on your way to deer camp for another season.

Until then, good hunting!

www.ingramcontent.com/pod-product-compliance
Lightning Source LLC
Chambersburg PA
CBHW020011050426
42450CB00005B/411